Here.	**Qui.** kōō·ē'.
There.	**Là.** lä.
On/To the right.	**A destra.** ä des'trä.
On/To the left.	**A sinistra.** ä sēnēs'trä.
Straight ahead.	**Sempre diritto.** sem'pre dērē'tō.
Do you have …?	**Ha …?** ä …?
I would like …	**Vorrei …** vōre'ē …
How much does this cost?	**Quanto costa?** kōō·än'tō kō'stä?
Could you please write that down for me?	**Me lo può scrivere, per favore?** me lō pōō·ō' skrē'vere, per fävō're?
Where is …?	**Dov'è …?** dōve' …?
Where *is/are* there …?	***Dov'è/Dove sono …?*** dōve'/dō've sō'nō …?
Today.	**Oggi.** ō'jē.
Tomorrow.	**Domani.** dōmä'nē.
I don't want to.	**Non voglio.** nōn vō'lyō.
I can't.	**Non posso.** nōn pō'sō.
Just a minute, please.	**Un momento, per favore!** oon mōmen'tō, per fävō're!
Leave me alone!	**Mi lasci in pace!** mē lä'shē ēn pä'tshe!

Name
Nome
Home address
Indirizzo di residenza

Date of birth
Data di nascita
Vacation address
Indirizzo di vacanza

ID/passport no.
Numero *della carta d'identità/del passaporto*

In case of emergency, please contact:
In caso di emergenza avvisare:

Important information (allergies, medicines, blood type, etc.)
**Informazioni importanti (allergie, farmaci,
gruppo sanguigno ecc.)**

In case of lost traveler's checks, please contact:

In case of lost credit cards, please contact:

Langenscheidt

Universal-Phrasebook Italian

Edited by the
Langenscheidt Editorial Staff

Langenscheidt

New York · Berlin · Munich · Vienna · Zurich

Phonetic transcriptions: The Glanze Intersound System
Illustrations: Kirill Chudinskiy

ISBN 978-1-58573-556-3
© 2006 Langenscheidt KG, Berlin and Munich
Printed in Germany

3. 4. 5. 6.   11 10 09 08 07

INHALT

5

7   ENTERTAINMENT AND SPORTS

10 TIME AND WEATHER

8

HOW TO FIND IT

This phrasebook contains all of the most important expressions and words you'll need for your trip. They have been divided up according to situation and organised into 10 chapters. The page borders have been colored to help you find things even more quickly.

Each chapter consists of example sentences and lists of words together with complementary vocabulary. This will help you put together exactly the right sentence you need for any situation. The easy-to-understand basic grammar section will give you further support.

Of course you can just show the person you're talking to the Italian translation of the sentence you wish to say. But the easily distinguished, blue phonetic alphabet will enable you to speak your chosen phrase without any knowledge of Italian whatsoever.

For vital situations we have also included sentences that go from Italian to English, so that an Italian may also be able to communicate with you.

In order to cover as many different situations as possible, we offer alternatives with many sentences; these are written in italics and separated by a slash:

Will I see you *tomorrow/this evening*?	**Ci vediamo *domani/stasera*?**
	tshē vedyä'mō *dōmän'ē/stäse'rä*?

9

You can separate the alternatives into individual sentences, asking either:

Will I see you tomorrow?	**Ci vediamo domani?**
	tshē vedyä'mō dōmän'ē?
or	
Will I see you this evening?	**Ci vediamo stasera?**
	tshē vedyä'mō stäse'rä?

When we offer more than two possibilities there will be an ellipsis at that point in the sentence; the possible phrases to complete your sentence will be listed underneath:

I would like...	**Vorrei...**
	vōre'ē...
a list of hotels.	**un annuario alberghi.**
	ōōn änōō·är'yō älber'gē.
a map of the area.	**una cartina della zona.**
	ōō'nä kärtē'nä de'lä dzō'nä.
a map of the city.	**una pianta della città.**
	ōō'nä pyän'tä de'lä tshētä'.
a map of the subway.	**una cartina della metropolitana.**
	ōō'nä kärtē'nä de'lä metrōpōlētä'nä.
a calendar of events.	**un programma delle manifestazioni.**
	ōōn prōgrä'mä de'le mänēfestätsyō'nē.

You can then put them together as needed, for example:

I would like a map of the city.	**Vorrei una pianta della città.**
	vōre'ē ōō'nä pyän'tä de'lä tshētä'.

10

Often you will also find sentence completions in parentheses. You can include these in your communication as you like.

How much does this cost (approximately)?	**Quanto costa (all'incirca)?**
	kōō·än'tō kō'stä (älēntshēr'kä)?

If you wish to know the exact price, then simply leave out the word for approximately - **all'incirca**.

In Italian the form of the word used is sometimes dependent upon the gender of either the person speaking or the person addressed. In these cases we have indicated the different forms by the symbols ♂ (masculine) and ♀ (feminine):

Are you married?	**È ♂ sposato/ ♀ sposata?**
	e ♂ spōzä'tō/ ♀ spōzä'tä?

You would ask a man: **È sposato?**, and a woman **È sposata?**

In Italian, nouns and their qualifying adjectives belong to either the masculine or feminine gender, and the articles differ accordingly. To clarify this we have used the abbreviations *m* for masculine and *f* for feminine words in the vocabulary lists. We have included the feminine endings with the adjectives only when they are irregular. You will find the rules for the regular endings in the short grammar section of this book.

We hope you enjoy using our phrasebook and have a fun-filled vacation!

HOW DO YOU PRONOUNCE IT?

All words and phrases are accompanied by simplified pronunciation. The sound symbols are the ones you are familiar with from your high-school or college dictionaries of the *English* language, but applied here to foreign languages – a unique feature of *Langenscheidt's Universal Phrasebooks.*

Symbol	Approximate Sound	Examples
	VOWELS	
ä	The *a* of *father.*	*facile* fä´tshēle
e	Either the *e* of *met* (as in Italian *festa*) or the *a* of *fate* (as in Italian *sera*). The difference is not shown here; it has to be learned by listening.	*festa* fe´stä *sera* se´rä
ē	The *e* of *he.*	*piccolo* pē´kōlō
ī	The *i* of *time.*	*dai* dī *traino* trī´no
ō	Either the *o* of *nose* (as in Italian *sole*) or the *o* of *often* (as in Italian *donna*). The difference is not shown here; it has to be learned by listening.	*sole* sō´le *donna* dō´nä

Symbol	Approximate Sound	Examples
oi	The *oi* of *voice*.	*poi* poi
o͞o	The *u* of *rule* (but without the "upglide").	*luna* lo͞o'nä
ou	The *ou* of *house*.	*laudare* loudä'rᵉ
CONSONANTS		
b	The *b* of *boy*.	*bello* be'lō
d	The *d* of *do*.	*dare* dä're
f	The *f* of *far*.	*farina* färē'nä
g	The *g* of *go*.	*gusto* go͞o'stō
j	The *j* of *John*.	*giorno* jōr'nō *oggetto* ōje'tō
k	The *k* of *key*, the *c* of *can*.	*casa* kä'sä *scherzo* sker'tsō
l	The *l* of *love* (not of *fall*).	*mela* me'lä
m	The *m* of *me*.	*mano* mä'nō
n	The *n* of *no*.	*nome* nō'me
ng	The *ng* of *sing*. (Occurs in some foreign words in Italian.)	*bowling* bō'lēng
p	The *p* of *pin*.	*pane* pä'ne

Symbol	Approximate Sound	Examples
r	The r of *run* (but with a slight "trill").	*roba* rō'bä *carta* kär'tä
s	The s of *sun* (See also z, below.)	*sala* sä'lä *casa* kä'sä
sh	The sh of *shine*.	*lasciare* läshä're
t	The t of *toy*.	*tempo* tem'pō
tsh	The ch of *much*.	*cento* tshen'tō
v	The v of *vat*.	*vita* vē'tä
y	The y of *year*.	*gennaio* jenä'yō *stiamo* styä'mō
z	The z of *zeal*.	*paese* pä·e'ze *sbaglio* zbä'lyō

Note these frequent combinations:

ly   as in *meglio* me'lyō
ny   as in *agnello* änye'lō or *legno* le'nyō
ts   as in *rizzare* rētsä're or *zampa* tsäm'pä
dz   as in *mezzo* me'dzō or *zebra* dze'brä
tsy   as in *negozio* negō'tsyō
ōō·e as in *guerra* gōō·e'rä
ōō·ē as in *qui* kōō·ē' or *guidare* gōō·ēdä're

A raised dot separates two neighboring vowel symbols. This dot is merely a convenience to the eye; it does not indicate a break in pronunciation.

Human Relations

HI AND BYE!

Good morning.	**Buongiorno!** bōō-ōnjōr'nō!
Good afternoon.	**Buongiorno!** bōō-ōnjōr'nō!
Good evening.	**Buona sera!** bōō-ō'nä se'rä!
Good night.	**Buona notte!** bōō-ō'nä nō'te!
Hi.	**Ciao!** tshäō!

INFO To greet someone during the late afternoon and evening, say **Buona sera**. **Buona notte** is used only very late in the evening before you go to bed. Say **Ciao** to greet good friends or acquaintances.

May I sit here?	**Posso sedermi accanto a Lei/te?** pō'sō seder'mē äkän'tō ä le'ē/te?
I'm sorry, but this seat is taken.	**No, mi dispiace, qui è già occupato.** nō, mē dēspyä'tshe, kōō-ē' e jä ōkōōpä'tō.
How are you?	**Come sta/stai?** kō'me stä/stī?
I'm sorry, but I have to go now.	**Mi dispiace, ma adesso devo andare.** mē dēspyä'tshe, mä äde'sō de'vō ändä're.
Good-bye!	**Arrivederci!** ärēveder'tshē!
So long/see you tomorrow!	**A presto/domani!** ä pre'stō/dōmä'nē!
Bye!	**Ciao!** tshäō!

16

INFO To take your leave of good friends you say **Ciao**. The more "official" way to say goodbye is **Arrivederci**, or **Arrivederla** ärēveder'lä if you wish to show particular respect to an individual person.

Nice meeting you.	**Molto piacere di aver La conosciuta/ averti conosciuto.** mōl'tō pyätshe're dē äver'lä kōnōshōō'tä/äver'tē kōnōshōō'tō.
Thank you for a lovely evening.	**Grazie per la bella serata.** grä'tsē·e per lä be'lä serä'tä.
Have a good trip!	**Buon viaggio!** bōō·ōn' vyä'jō!

SMALL TALK ...

... about yourself and others

What's your name?	**Come si chiama/ti chiami?** Kō'me sē kyä'mä/tē kyä'mē?
My name is ...	**Mi chiamo ...** mē kyä'mō ...

INFO There are three ways to say "you" in Italian: a familiar, a polite, and a plural form. The **tu** tōō (familiar) form is used when friends, children, and young people talk individually to each other. Use the **Lei** le'ē (polite) form when speaking to strangers, lesser-known acqua... elders. And when addressing two or more people – ... how well you know them – use the **voi** vo'ē (plural) f...

Where are you from?	**Di *dov'è/dove sei*?** dē dōve'/dō've se'ē?
I'm from the United States.	**Sono ♂ americano/♀ americana.** sō'nō ♂ ämerēkä'nō/♀ ämerēkä'nä.
I'm from New York.	**Sono di New York.** sō'nō dē nōōyōrk'.
Are you married?	**È/Sei ♂ sposato/♀ sposata?** e/se'ē ♂ spōzä'tō/♀ spōzä'tä?
Do you have children?	**Ha/Hai figli?** ä/ī fē'lyē?
Do you have any brothers or sisters?	**Ha/Hai dei fratelli?** ä/ī de'ē fräte'lē?
I have a *sister/brother*.	**Ho *una sorella/un fratello*.** ō ōō'nä sōre'lä/ōōn fräte'lō.
How old are you?	**Quanti anni *ha/hai*?** kōō·än'tē ä'nē ä/ī?
I'm … old.	**Ho … anni.** ō … ä'nē.
What sort of work do you do?	**Che lavoro *fa/fai*?** ke lävō'rō fä/fī?
I'm still going to school.	**Vado ancora a scuola.** vä'dō änkō'rä ä skōō-ō'lä.

... about home and vacation

? **È la prima volta che *è*/*sei* qui?**
e lä prēmä vōl'tä ke *e*/*se'ē* kōō·ē'?

Is this your first ... here?

No, I've been to Italy ... time(s) before.

No, sono ♂*stato*/♀*stata* in Italia già altre ... volte. nō, sō'nō ♂stä'tō/♀stä'tä ēn ētä'lyä jä al'tre ... vōl'te.

? **Da quanto tempo *è*/*sei* qui?**
dä kōō·än'tō tem'pō *e*/*se'ē* kōō·ē'?

How long have you been here?

For ... *days*/*weeks* now.

Da ... *giorni*/*settimane*.
dä ... jōr'nē/setēmä'ne.

? **Per quanto tempo *rimane*/*rimani* ancora?** per kōō·än'tō tem'pō *rēmä'ne*/*rēmä'nē* änkō'rä?

How much longer will you be staying?

I'm leaving tomorrow.

Riparto domani. rēpär'tō dōmä'nē.

Another *week*/*two weeks*.

Ancora *una settimana*/*due settimane*. änkō'rä *ōō'nä setēmä'nä*/*dōō'e setēmä'ne.*

? **_Le_/_Ti_ piace qui?**
le/tē pyä'tshe kōō·ē'?

How do you like it here?

I like it very much.

Mi piace molto. mē pyä'tshe mōl'tō.

Have you seen ... ?

_Ha_/_Hai_ già visto ...? ä/ījä vē'stō ...

1

19

Have you ever been to America?	**È/Sei** ♂ **stato/** ♀ **stata mai in America?** e/se'ē ♂ stä'tō/ ♀ stä'tä mī ēn äme'rēkä?
Did you like it there?	**Le/Ti è piaciuta?** le/tē e pyätshōō'tä?
You should visit me if you come to America.	**Mi** *venga/vieni* **a trovare, se** *viene/vieni* **in America.** mē ven'gä/vye'nē ä trōvä're, se vye'ne/vye'nē ēn äme'rēkä.
This is my address.	**Ecco il mio indirizzo.** e'kō ēl mē'ō ēndērē'tsō.
You're welcome to stay at my house.	**Può/Puoi venire a stare da me.** pōō·o'/pōō·oi' venē're ä stä're dä me.
I'd love to show you the *city/town*.	**Le/Ti faccio vedere la città.** le/tē fä'tshō vede're lä tshētä'.

SOCIALIZING

Would you like to …?

What are you doing tomorrow?	**Che cosa** *fa/fai* **domani?** ke kō'sä fä/fī dōmä'nē?
We could do something together, if you like.	**Potremmo fare qualcosa insieme, se** *Le/ti* **va.** pōtre'mō fä're kōō·älkō'sä ēnsye'me, se le/tē vä.
Shall we meet *this evening/tomorrow?*	**Ci vediamo** *stasera/domani?* tshē vedyä'mō stäse'rä/dōmä'nē?

Yes, I'd like that.	**Sì, volentieri.** sē, võlentye′rē.
I'm sorry, but I already have plans.	**Purtroppo non posso, ho già un impegno.** pōōrtrō′pō nōn pō′sō, ō jä ōōn ēmpe′nyō.

INFO When addressing a man, use **signor** sēnyör and his last name, if known. Women are addressed as **signora** sēnyö′rä, girls and younger women as **signorina** sēnyōrē′nä, with or without the last name.

Would you like to join me for dinner this evening?	**Andiamo a mangiare insieme stasera?** ändyä′mō ä mänjä′re ēnsye′me stäse′rä?

➡ *see also: Dining with Friends (p. 115),*
Going out in the Evening (p. 193)

I'd like to invite you to …	*La/Ti* vorrei invitare. lä/tē vōre′ē ēnvētä′re.
When/Where shall we meet?	*Quando/Dove* ci incontriamo? kōō·än′dō/dō′ve tshē ēnkōntrē·ä′mō?
Let's meet at … o'clock.	**Incontriamoci alle …** ēnkōntrē·ämōtshē ä′le …
I'll pick you up at … o'clock.	*La/Ti* vengo a prendere alle … lä/tē ven′gō ä pren′dcre ä′le …
I'll take you home.	*La/Ti* accompagno a casa. lä/tē äkompä′nyō ä kä′sä.

21

| Will I see you again? | **Ci vediamo un'altra volta?** |
| | tshē vedyä′mō ōōnäl′trä vōl′tä? |

No, thanks!

| I'm afraid that won't be possible. | **Mi dispiace, ma non posso.** |
| | mē dēspyä′tshe, mä nōn pô′sō. |

| I already have plans. | **Ho già un impegno.** |
| | ō jä ōōn ēmpe′nyō. |

| I'm waiting for someone. | **Aspetto qualcuno.** äspe′tō kōō·älkōō′nō. |

| I'm not interested. | **Non ho voglia.** nōn ō vō′lyä. |

| That's enough of that! | **Adesso basta!** äde′sō bä′stä! |

| Get lost! | **Sparisci!** spärē′shē! |

COMMUNICATING

| Does anyone here speak English? | **C'è qualcuno che parla inglese?** tshe kōō·älkōō′nō ke pär′lä ēn·gle′se? |

| **?** **Parla/Parli italiano?** pär′lä/pär′lē ētälyä′nō? | Do you speak Italian? |

| Only a little. | **Soltanto un po'.** sōltän′tō ōōn pô. |

| Please speak a little more slowly. | **Per favore, parli più lentamente.** per fävô′re, pär′lē pyōō lentämen′te. |

? *Ha/Hai capito?* ä/ī käpē'tō?　　Do you understand?

I understand.	**Ho capito.** ō käpē'tō.	

I didn't understand that. **Non ho capito questo.** nōn ō käpē'tō kōō·e'stō.

Could you repeat that, please? **Lo può ripetere, per favore?** lō pōō·ō' rēpe'tere, per fävō're?

What is this called in Italian? **Come si dice in italiano?** kō'me sē dē'tshe ēn ētälyä'nō?

What does … mean? **Che cosa significa …?** ke kō'sä sēnyē'fēkä …?

Please write it down for me. **Me lo scriva, per favore.** me lō skrē'vä, per fävō're?

How do you pronounce that? **Come si pronuncia?** kō'me sē pronōōn'tshä?

What do you think?

It *was/is* very nice here. **È stato/È molto bello qui.** e stä'tō/e mōl'tō be'lō kōō·ē'.

Great! **Benissimo!** benē'sēmō!

Wonderful! **Magnifico!** mänyē'fēkō!

I like that. **Mi piace.** mē pyä'tshe.

Gladly. **Molto volentieri.** mōl'tō vōlentye'rē.

OK. **Va bene.** vä be'ne.

It's all the same to me.	**Mi è indifferente.** mē e ēndēferen'te.
Whatever you like.	**Come *vuole/vuol.*** kō'me *vōō·ō'le/vōō·ōl!*
I don't know yet.	**Non lo so ancora.** nōn lō sō änkō'rä.
Maybe.	**Forse.** fōr'se.
Too bad!	**Che peccato!** ke pekä'tō!
I'm afraid that's impossible.	**Purtroppo non è possibile.** pōōrtrō'pō nōn e pōse'bēle.
I'd rather …	**Preferirei …** preferēre'ē …
I don't like that.	**Non mi piace.** nōn mē pyä'tshe.
No.	**No.** nō.
Absolutely not.	**In nessun caso.** ēn nesōōn' kä'zō.

BASIC PHRASES

Please; Thank you

Could you please help me?	**Mi potrebbe aiutare, per favore?** mē pōtre'be äyōōtä're, per favō're?
Yes, please.	**Sì, volentieri.** sē, vōlentye'rē.
No, thank you.	**No, grazie.** nō, grä'tsē·e.
Thank you very much.	**Grazie mille.** grä'tsē·e mē'le.

24

| Thank you, that was very nice of you. | **Molte grazie, è stato molto gentile da parte Sua.** mõl'te grä'tsē·e, e stä'tō mōl'tō jentē'le dä pär'te sōō'ä. |
| You're welcome. | **Prego.** pre'gō. |

INFO To say "please," use **per favore**. The Italian word **prego** means "you're welcome" when used as a response to **grazie** (thank you). It is, however, also used when giving or handing something to someone (like saying "Here you are") or indicating to someone to take a seat or go ahead ("After you").

| May I? | **Posso?** pō'sō? |

I'm sorry!

Excuse me!	**Scusi!** skōō'zē!
Sorry about that.	**Mi dispiace.** mē dēspyä'tshe.
It was a misunderstanding.	**È stato un malinteso.** e stä'tō ōōn mälente'zō.

Best wishes!

Best wishes!	**Tante belle cose!** tän'te be'le kō'sē!
Happy birthday!	**Tanti auguri di buon compleanno!** tän'tē ougōō'rē dē bōō·ōn' kōmple·ä'nō!
Have a good trip!	**Buon viaggio!** bōō·ōn' vyä'jō!

25

Have a good time!	**Buon divertimento!** bōō·ōn' dĕvĕrtēmĕn'tō!
Merry Christmas!	**Buon Natale!** bōō·ōn' nätä'le!
Happy New Year!	**Felice anno nuovo!** felē'tshe ä'nō nōō·ō'vō!
Happy holidays!	**Buone feste!** bōō·ō'ne fe'ste!

FOR THE HANDICAPPED

I'm physically handicapped. Can you please help me?	**Sono ♂ handicappato/♀ handicappata. Mi può aiutare, per favore?** sō'nō ♂ ändēkäpä'tō/♀ ändēkäpä'tä. mē pōō·ō' äyōōtä're, per fävō're?
Do you have a wheelchair for me?	**Ha una sedia a rotelle per me?** ä ōō'nä se'dyä ä rōte'le per me?
Can you please take my luggage to the *room/taxi*?	**Mi può portare i bagagli *in camera/fino al taxi*?** mē pōō·ō' pōrtä're ē bägä'lyē *ēn kä'merä/fē'nō äl tä'ksē*?
Where is the nearest elevator?	**Dov'è l'ascensore più vicino?** dōve' läshensō're pyōō vētshē'nō?
Is it suitable for wheelchairs?	**È accessibile alle sedie a rotelle?** e ätshese'bēle ä'le se'dye ä rōte'le?
Is there a ramp for wheelchairs?	**C'è una salita per sedie a rotelle?** tshe ōō'nä säle'tä per se'dye ä rōte'le?

26

| Where is the rest room for handicapped? | **Dov'è un gabinetto per handicappati?** dōve' ōōn gäbēne'tō per ändēkäpä'tē? | |
| I need someone to accompany me. | **Ho bisogno di qualcuno che mi accompagni.** ō bēzō'nyō dē kōō·älkōō·nō ke mē äkōmpä'nyē. | **1** |

Human Relations

address	**l'indirizzo** lēndērē'tsō
alone	**solo** sō'lō
to arrive	**arrivare** ärēvä're
boyfriend	**il ragazzo** ēl rägä'tsō
brother	**il fratello** ēl fräte'lō
brothers and sisters	**i fratelli** ē fräte'lē
child	**il bambino** ēl bämbē'nō
city	**la città** lä tshētä'
to go dancing	**andare a ballare** ändä're ä bälä're
daughter	**la figlia** lä fē'lyä
father	**il padre** ēl pä'dre
friend *(male)*	**l'amico** lämē'kō
friend *(female)*	**l'amica** lämē'kä
girlfriend	**la ragazza** lä rägä'tsä
to have plans	**avere un impegno** äve're ōōn ēmpe'nyō
husband	**il marito** ēl märē'tō
to invite	**invitare** ēnvētä're
to like *(I would like to)*	**volere** vōle'ro
to like *(it appeals to me)*	**piacere** pyä'tshere

to leave	**partire** pärtē're
little	**poco** pō'ko
to make a date	**darsi appuntamento** där'sē äpōōntämen'tō
married	***sposato/sposata*** spōzä'tō/spōzä'tä
to meet *(get to know)*	**conoscere** kōnō'shere
to meet *(up with someone)*	**incontrarsi** ēnkōnträr'sē
mother	**la madre** lä mä'dre
no	**no** nō
to go out to eat	**andare a mangiare (fuori)** ändä're ä mänjä're (fōō-ō'rē)
profession	**la professione** lä prōfesyō'ne
satisfied	**contento** kōnten'tō
school	**la scuola** lä skōō-ō'lä
sister	**la sorella** lä sōre'lä
son	**il figlio** ēl fē'lyō
to speak	**parlare** pärlä're
student *(female)*	**la studentessa** lä stōōdente'sä
student *(male)*	**lo studente** lō stōōden'te
to study	**studiare** stōōdyä're
to understand	**capire** käpē're
vacation	**la vacanza** lä väkän'tsä
to wait	**aspettare** äspetä're
wife	**la moglie** lä mō'lye
to write down	**scrivere** skrē'vere
yes	**sì** sē

28

BUSINESS CONTACTS

On the Phone

➡ see also: Communicating (p. 22)

This is *(name)*
at/from *(company)*.

Qui parla ... della ditta ...
kōō-ē' pär'lä ... de'lä dē'tä ...

I would like to speak
to ...

Vorrei parlare con ...
vōre'ē pärlä're kōn ...

! **Sono io.** sō'nō ē'ō. — Speaking.

! **Glielo/Gliela passo.**
• lye'lō/lye'lä pä'sō. — I'll connect you.

! **Attenda in linea, per favore.**
äten'dä ēn lē'ne·ä, per fävō're. — Please hold.

! **... è occupato.**
• ... e ōkōōpä'tō. — ... is busy at the moment.

! **... oggi non c'è.** ... ō'jē nōn tshe. — ... is not here today.

? **Vuole lasciare detto qualcosa?**
• vōō·ō'le läshä're de'tō kōō·älkō'sä? — Would you like to leave a message?

May I leave a
message for ...?

Posso lasciare un messaggio per ...?
pō'sō läshä're ōōn mesä'jō per ...?

At the Reception Desk

I'm here to see Mr. Rossi.	**Vorrei andare dal signor Rossi.** vōre'ē ändä're däl sēnyōr' rō'sē.
My name is ...	**Il mio nome è ...** ēl mē'ō nō'me e ...
I have an appointment with ... at ... o'clock.	**Ho un appuntamento con ... alle ...** ō ōōn äpōōntämen'tō kōn ... ä'le ...

!	**Un momento, per favore.** ōōn mōmen'tō, per fävō're.	One moment, please.
!	**... arriva subito.** ... äre'vä sōō'bētō.	... will be right here.
!	**... è ancora ad una riunione.** ... e änkō'rä äd ōō'nä rē-ōōnēō'ne.	... is still in a meeting.
!	**Venga, La accompagno da ...** ven'gä, lä äkōmpä'nyō dä ...	Please follow me. I'll show you to ...
?	**Può attendere un istante, per favore?** pōō-ō' äten'dere ōōn ēstän'te, per fävō're?	Would you please wait here a moment?

At Trade Fairs

I'm looking for the ... booth.	**Cerco lo stand della ditta ...** tsher'kō lō ständ de'lä dē'tä ...
Do you have any brochures on ...?	**Ha del materiale informativo su ...?** ä del mäteryä'le ēnfōrmätē'vō sōō ...?

| Do you also have pamphlets in English? | **Avete dei depliant anche in inglese?** ave´te de´ē deplē·än´ än´ke ēn ēn·gle´se? |
| Whom can I ask? | **A chi mi posso rivolgere?** ä kē mē pō´sō rēvōl´jere. |

Business Contacts

address	**l'indirizzo** lēndērē´tsō
to announce oneself	**annunciare** änōōntshyä´re
appointment	**l'appuntamento** läpōōntämen´tō
auditorium	**il padiglione** ēl pädēlyō´ne
booth	**lo stand** lō ständ
to call (on the phone)	**telefonare** telefōnä´re
catalog	**il catalogo** ēl kätä´lōgō
client, customer	**il cliente** ēl klē·en´te
company	**la ditta** lä dē´tä
conference	**la conferenza** lä kōnferen´tsä
– room	**la sala delle riunioni** lä sä´lä de´le rē·ōōnēō´nē
copy	**la fotocopia** lä fōtōkō´pyä
corporation	**il gruppo industriale** ēl grōō´pō ēndōōstrē·ä´le
department	**Il reparto** el repär´tō
– head	**il direttore del reparto** el dēretō´re del repär´tō

31

documents	**la documentazione** lä dōkōōmentätsyō'ne
entrance	**l'entrata** lenträ'tä
exit	**l'uscita** lōōshē'tä
fax machine	**il telefax** ēl te'lefäks
information	**l'informazione** *f* lēnfōrmätsyō'ne
interpreter	**l'interprete** *m, f* lēnter'prete
management	**la direzione** lä dēretsyō'ne
manager	**il direttore** ēl dēretō're
to meet (up with someone)	**incontrare** ēnkōnträ're
meeting *(discussion)*	**la riunione** lä rē-ōōnyō'ne
meeting *(get-together)*	**l'incontro** lēnkōn'trō
news	**il messaggio** ēl mesä'jō
to notify	**avvisare** ävēsä're
office	**l'ufficio** lōōfē'tshō
price	**il prezzo** ēl pre'tsō
– list	**il listino prezzi** ēl lēstē'nō pre'tsē
prospectus	**il depliant** ēl deplē-än'
reception	**la reception** lä resep'shōn
representative	**il rappresentante** ēl räpresentän'te
sample	**il campione** ēl kämpyo'ne
secretary	**la segretaria** lä segretär'yä
subsidiary	**la (società) filiale** lä (sōtshetä') fēlyä'le
telephone	**il telefono** ēl tele'fōnō
to telephone	**telefonare** telefōnä're
trade fair	**la fiera** lä fye'rä

32

Accommodations

INFORMATION

Where is the tourist information office?	**Dov'è l'ufficio informazioni turistiche?** dōve' lōōfē'tshō ēnfōrmätsyō'nē tōōrē'stēke?
Do you know where I can rent a room here?	**Mi saprebbe dire dove posso trovare una camera?** mē säpre'be dē're dō've pō'sō trōvä're ōō'nä kä'merä?

INFO The Tourist Information Office (**ufficio informazioni turistiche**) will be happy to give you information about hotels, guest houses, or rooms to rent in family homes.

Could you recommend …	**Mi potrebbe consigliare …** mē pōtre'be kōnsēlyä're …
a good hotel?	**un buon albergo?** ōōn bōō·ōn' älber'gō?
an inexpensive hotel?	**un albergo economico?** ōōn älber'gō ekōnō'mēkō?
a boarding house?	**una pensione?** ōō'nä pensyō'ne?
a room at a private home?	**un alloggio presso privati?** ōōn älō'jō pre'sō prēvä'tē?
I'm looking for somewhere to stay …	**Cerco un alloggio …** tsher'kō ōōn älō'jō …
in a *central/quiet* location.	**in *centro/una zona tranquilla.*** ēn *tshen'trō/ōō'nä dzō'nä tränkōō·ē'lä.*

34

at the beach.	**vicino alla spiaggia.**
	vē̇tshē'nō ä'lä spyä'jä.
What will it cost (approximately)?	**Quanto costa (all'incirca)?**
	kōō·än'tō kō'stä (älēntshēr'kä)?
Can you make a reservation for me there?	**Mi può fare una prenotazione?**
	mē pōō·o' fä're ōō'nä prenōtätsyō'ne?
Is there a *youth hostel/camping ground* here?	**C'è un *ostello della gioventù/campeggio* qui vicino?** tshe ōōn ōste'lō de'lä jōventōō'/kämpe'jō kōō·e' vētshē'nō?
Is it far from here?	**È lontano da qui?** e lōntä'nō dä kōō·e'?
How do I get there?	**Come ci si arriva?** kō'me tshē sē äre'vä?
Can you draw me a map?	**Mi può fare uno schizzo della strada da fare?** mē pōō·o' fä're ōō'nō ske'tsō de'lä strä'dä dä fä're?

HOTEL AND VACATION RENTAL

Hotel

| I have a reservation. My name is … | **Ho una camera prenotata qui da voi. Il mio nome è …** ō ōō'nä kä'merä prenō-tä'tä kōō·e' dä voi. ōl mē'ō no'me e … |
| Here is my confirmation. | **Ecco la conferma.** e'kō lä kōnfer'mä. |

35

INFO If you would like a double room, you have a choice between a **camera matrimoniale** kä´merä mätrēmōnēä´le (a room with a double bed) and a **camera doppia** kä´merä dō´pyä (a room with two single beds).

Do you have a *double/single* room available …	**Avete una camera *doppia/singola* libera …** äve´te ōō´nä kä´merä dō´pyä/ sēn´gōlä lē´berä …
for *one night/* … *nights*?	**per *una notte/*… *notti*?** per ōō´nä nō´te/… nō´tē?
with a *full bathroom/shower and toilet*?	**con *bagno/doccia e WC*?** kōn bä´nyō/dō´tshä e vōō–tshē´?
with a sea view?	**con vista sul mare?** kōn ve´stä sōōl mä´re?
with a balcony?	**con balcone?** kōn bälkō´ne?

! **Purtroppo è tutto esaurito.** pōōrtrō´pō e tōō´tō ezä·ōōrē´tō.	I'm sorry, but we're booked out.

! **Domani/Il … si libererà una camera.** dōmä´nē/ēl … sē lēbererä´ ōō´nä kä´merä.	*Tomorrow/On …* there will be a room available.

How much will it cost …	**Quanto costa …** kōō·än´tō kō´stä …
with/without breakfast?	**con/senza la prima colazione?** kōn/sen´tsä lä prē´mä kōlätsyō´ne?

36

with half board/full board included?	**a mezza pensione/pensione completa?** ä me'tsä pensyō'ne/ pensyō'ne kômple'tä?
Is there a discount for children?	**C'è una riduzione per i bambini?** tshē ōō'nä rēdōōtsyō'ne per ē bämbē'nē?
May I have a look at the room?	**Posso vederc la camera?** pô'sō vede're lä kä'merä?
Do you have a … room?	**Avete una camera …** äve'te ōō'nä kä'merä …
less expensive	**più economica?** pyōō ekōnô'mēkä?
larger	**più grande?** pyōō grän'de?
quieter	**più tranquilla?** pyōō tränkōō·ē'lä?
It's very nice. I'll take it.	**È molto bella, la prendo.** e môl'tō be'lä, lä pren'dō.

? Ha dei bagagli? ä de'ē bägä'lyē?   Do you have any luggage?

Can you have a crib put in the room?	**Si può aggiungere un lettino per bambini?** sē pōō·ô' äjōōn'jere ōōn letē'nō per bämbē'nē?
Where are the showers?	**Dove sono le docce?** dō've sō'nō le dō'tshe?
Where can I park my car?	**Dove posso mettere la macchina?** dō've pô'sō met'ere lä mä'kēnä?

37

Where is the *dining/breakfast* room?	**Dov'è la sala *da pranzo/della prima colazione*?** döve' lä sä'lä dä prän'tsö/de'lä prē'mä kölätsyö'ne?
Can I have breakfast in my room?	**È possibile fare colazione in camera?** e pöse'bële fä're kölätsyö'ne ën kä'merä?
Can I give you my valuables for safe-keeping?	**Le posso lasciare in custodia i miei oggetti di valore?** le pö'sö läshä're ën kööstö'dyä ē mye'ē öje'tē dē välö're?
I'd like to pick up my valuables.	**Vorrei ritirare i miei oggetti di valore.** vöre'ē rētērä're ē mye'ē öje'tē dē välö're.
Can you exchange money for me?	**Mi potete cambiare dei soldi?** mē pöte'te kämbyä're de'ē söl'dē?
I'd like the key to room ...	**La chiave della camera ..., per favore.** lä kyä've de'lä kä'merä ..., per fävö're.
Can I make a call to America (from my room)?	**Posso chiamare in America (dal telefono in camera)?** pö'sö kyämä're ën äme'rëkä (däl tele'fönö ën kä'merä)?
Is there any mail/Are there any messages for me?	**C'è *posta/un messaggio* per me?** tshe pö'stä/ōōn mesä'jö per me?
I'd like a wakeup call at ... o'clock (tomorrow morning), please.	**Per favore, mi svegli (domani mattina) alle ...** per fävö're, mē sve'lyē (dōmä'nē mätē'nä) ä'le ...

We're leaving tomorrow.	**Partiamo domattina.**
	pärtyä'/mō dōmätē'nä.
Would you please prepare my bill?	**Prepari il conto, per favore.**
	prepä're ēl kōn'tō, per fävō're.
I/We really liked it here.	**È stato davvero piacevole qui.**
	e stä'tō däve'rō pyätshe'vōle kōō-ē'.
May I leave my luggage here until … o'clock?	**Posso lasciare qui i miei bagagli fino alle …?**
	pō'sō läshä're kōō-ē' ē mye'ē bägä'lye fē'nō ä'le …?
Would you call a taxi for me, please?	**Mi chiama un taxi, per favore?**
	mē kyä'mä ōōn tä'ksē, per fävō're?

Vacation Rental

We have rented the apartment …	**Abbiamo preso in affitto l'appartamento …** äbyä'mō pre'sō ēn äfē'tō läpärtämen'tō …
Where can we pick up the keys to the apartment?	**Dove possiamo ritirare le chiavi dell'appartamento?** dō've pōsyä'mō rētērä're le kyä'vē deläpärtämen'tō?
Could you please explain how the … works?	**Per favore, ci potrebbe spiegare come funziona …** per fävō're, tshē pōtre'be spyegä're kō'me fōōntsyō'nä …
stove	**la cucina elettrica?** lä kōōtshē'nä ele'trēkä?
dishwasher	**la lavastoviglie?** lä lävästōvē'lye?

39

washing machine	**la lavatrice?** lä lävätrē'tshe?

Where do we put the trash?	**Dove si getta la spazzatura?** dō've sē je'tä lä spätsätōō'rä?

Where is the fuse box?	**Dove sono le valvole?** dō've sō'nō le väl'vōle?

Where is the meter?	**Dov'è il contatore?** dōve' ēl kōntätō're?

Where can I make a phone call?	**C'è un telefono qui?** tshe ōōn tele'fōnō kōō-ē'?

Can you please tell us where ... is?	**Ci saprebbe dire dov'è ...** tshē säpre'be dē're dove' ...
a bakery	**una panetteria?** ōō'nä päneterē'ä?
the nearest bus stop	**la fermata dell'autobus più vicina?** lä fermä'tä delou'tōbōōs pyōō vētshē'nä?
a butcher	**una macelleria?** ōō'nä mätshelerē'ä?
a grocery store	**un negozio di alimentari?** ōōn negō'tsyō dē älēmentä'rē?

Complaints

➡ *see also Please; Thank you (p. 24)*

The *shower*/*heating* doesn't work.	**La doccia/Il riscaldamento non funziona.** lä dō'tshä/ēl rēskäldämen'tō nōn fōōntsyō'nä.

The toilet doesn't flush.	**Lo sciacquone non funziona.** lō shäkōō·ō'ne nōn fōōntsyō'nä.
The window doesn't open/close.	**La finestra non si apre/chiude.** lä fēne'strä nōn sē ä'pre/kyōō'de.
Could I please have ...	**Per favore, potrei avere ancora ...** per fävō're, pōtre'ē ä've'rc änkō'ra ...
another blanket?	**una coperta?** ōō'nä kōper'tä?
some more dish towels?	**degli strofinacci da cucina?** de'lyē strōfēnä'tshe dä kōōtshē'nä?
another towel?	**un asciugamano?** ōōn äshōōgämä'nō?
a few more clothes hangers?	**un paio di attaccapanni?** ōōn pä'yō dē ätäkäpä'nē?
The light doesn't work.	**La luce non funziona.** La lōō'tshe nōn fōōntsyō'nä.
There's no (hot) water.	**Non c'è acqua (calda).** nōn tshe ä'kōō·ä (käl'dä).
The drain/The toilet is stopped up.	*Il tubo di scarico/Il gabinetto è intasato.* ēl tōō'bō dē skä'rēkō/ēl gäbēne'tō e ēntäsä'tō.

Hotel and Vacation Rental

adapter	**il riduttore.** ēl rēdōōtō're
additional costs	**le spese di mantenimento** le spe'se dē mäntenēmen'tō
apartment	**l'appartamento** läpärtämen'tō
ashtray	**il posacenere** ēl pōsätshe'nere

41

balcony	**il balcone** ēl bälkō'ne
bathroom	**il bagno** ēl bä'nyō
bathtub	**la vasca da bagno** lä väs'kä dä bä'nyō
beach umbrella	**l'ombrellone** *m* lōmbrelō'ne
bed	**il letto** ēl le'tō
-side lamp	**la lampada del comodino** lä läm'pädä del kōmōdē'nō
bedspread	**il copriletto** ēl kōprēle'tō
bill	**il conto** ēl kōn'tō
blanket	**la coperta di lana** lä kōper'tä dē lä'nä
breakfast	**la colazione** lä kōlätsyō'ne
– buffet	**il buffet della colazione** ēl bōōfe' de'lä kōlätsyō'ne
broken	**rotto** rō'tō
broom	**la scopa** lä skō'pä
cabin	**il bungalow** ēl bōōn'gälō
chair	**la sedia** lä se'dyä
cleaning products	**il detersivo** ēl detersē'vō
closet	**l'armadietto** lärmädye'tō
complaint	**il reclamo** ēl reklä'mō
crib	**il lettino (per bambini)** ēl letē'nō (per bämbē'nē)
cup	**la tazza** lä tä'tsä
departure	**la partenza** lä pärten'tsä
dining room	**la sala da pranzo** lä sä'lä dä prän'tsō
dinner	**la cena** lä tshe'nä
dirty	**sporco** spōr'kō
dishes	**i piatti** ē pyä'tē
dishwasher	**la lavastoviglie** lä lävästōvē'lye

door	**la porta** lä pōr'tä
– lock	**la serratura** lä serätōō'rä
double room	**la camera doppia** lä kä'merä dō'pyä
electricity	**la corrente** lä kören'te
elevator	**l'ascensore** *m* läshensō're
fan	**il ventilatore** el ventēlätō're
faucet	**il rubinetto (dell'acqua)**
	el rōōbēne'tō (delä'kōō-ä)
final cleaning	**la pulizia finale** lä pōōlētsē'ä fēnä'le
first floor	**il pianterreno** el pyäntere'nō
floor *(story)*	**il piano** el pyä'nō
flush	**lo sciacquone** lo shäkōō-ō'ne
full room and board	**la pensione completa**
	lä pensyō'ne kōmple'tä
fuse	**la valvola di sicurezza**
	lä väl'vōlä dē sēkōōre'tsä
gas cylinder	**la bombola del gas**
	lä bōm'bōlä del gäs
glass	**il bicchiere** el bēkye're
half room and board	**la mezza pensione** lä me'tsä pensyō'ne
high season	**l'alta stagione** läl'tä stäjō'ne
hotel	**l'hotel** *m*, **l'albergo** lōtel', lälber'gō
house	**la casa** lä kä'sä
key	**la chiave** lä kyä've
lamp	**la lampada** lä läm'pädä
light	**la luce** lä lōō'tshe
– bulb	**la lampadina** lä lämpädē'nä
– switch	**l'interruttore** *m* lēnterōōtō're

2

43

linens	**la biancheria da letto**
	lä byänkerē'ä dä le'tō
lost	**perso** per'sō
low season	**la fine stagione** lä fē'ne stäjō'ne
luggage	**i bagagli** ē bägä'lye
lunch	**il pranzo** ēl prän'tsō
maid	**la cameriera** lä kämerye'rä
mattress	**il materasso** ēl mäterä'sō
mirror	**lo specchio** lō spe'kyō
mosquito net	**la zanzariera** lä dzändzärye'rä
outlet	**la presa di corrente**
	lä pre'sä dē kōren'te
overnight stay	**il pernottamento** ēl pernōtämen'tō
pillow	**il cuscino** ēl kōōshē'nō
plate	**il piatto** ēl pyä'tō
plug	**la spina** lä spē'nä
pool	**la piscina** lä pēshē'nä
pre-season	**l'inizio stagione** *f* lēnē'tsyō stäjō'ne
reception	**la reception** lä rēsep'shōn
refrigerator	**il frigorifero** ēl frēgōrē'ferō
registration	**la registrazione** lä rejēsträtsyō'ne
rent	**l'affitto** läfē'tō
to rent	**prendere in affitto** pren'dere ēn äfē'tō
to reserve	**prenotare** prenōtä're
reserved	**prenotato** prenōtä'tō
room	**la camera** lä kä'merä
safe	**la cassaforte** lä käsäfōr'te
sheet	**il lenzuolo** ēl lentsōō-ō'lō
shower	**la doccia** lä dō'tshä

single room	**la camera singola** lä kä'merä sēn'gōlä
sink	**il lavandino** ēl lävändē'nō
stairs	**la scala** lä skä'lä
table	**il tavolo** ēl tä'vōlō
tax on visitors	**la tassa di soggiorno** lä tä'sä dē sōjōr'nō
telephone	**il telefono** ēl tele'fōnō
terrace	**la terrazza** lä terä'tsä
toilet	**il gabinetto** ēl gäbēne'tō
– paper	**la carta igienica** lä kär'tä ēje'nēkä
towel	**l'asciugamano** läshōōgämä'nō
trash container	**il bidone della spazzatura** ēl bēdō'ne de'lä spätsätōō'rä
trash can	**il secchio della spazzatura** ēl se'kyō de'lä spätsätōō'rä
TV room	**la sala della televisione** lä sä'lä de'lä televēzyō'ne
voltage	**il voltaggio** ēl vōltä'jo
to wake	**svegliare** svelyä're
water	**l'acqua** lä'kōō·ä
cold –	**l'acqua fredda** lä'kōō·ä fre'dä
hot –	**l'acqua calda** lä'kōō·ä käl'dä
window	**la finestra** lä fēne'strä
to work (function)	**funzionare** fōōntsyōnä're

45

YOUTH HOSTEL, CAMPING

Youth Hostel

Is there any room available?	**C'è ancora un posto libero?** tshe änkō'rä ōōn pō'stō lĕ'berō?
I would like to stay for *one night/... nights.*	**Vorrei rimanere per *una notte/... notti.*** vōre'ĕ rēmäne're per ōō'nä nō'te/... nō'tē.
How much will it cost for one night (per person)?	**Quanto costa il pernottamento (a persona)?** kōō-än'tō kō'stä ĕl pernōtämen'tō (ä persō'nä)?
Do you also have double rooms?	**Avete anche delle camere doppie?** äve'te än'ke de'le kä'mere dō'pye?
Is breakfast included?	**È compresa la prima colazione?** e kōmpre'sä lä prē'mä kōlätsyō'ne?
How much does ... cost?	**Quanto costa ...** kōō-än'tō kō'stä ...
breakfast	**la prima colazione?** lä prē'mä kōlätsyō'ne?
lunch	**il pranzo?** ĕl prän'tsō?
dinner	**la cena?** lä tshe'nä?
Where is the dining room?	**Dov'è la sala da pranzo?** dōve' lä sä'lä dä prän'tsō
When are the meals served?	**A che ora si mangia?** ä ke ō'rä sē män'jä?

Where can I buy something *to eat*/ *to drink*?	**Dov'è che si può comprare qualcosa da *mangiare/bere*?** dōve' ke sē pōō-ō' kōmprä're kōō-älkō'sä da *mänjä're/be're*?
Where are the bathrooms?	**Dove sono i bagni?** dō've sō'nō ē bä'nyē?
Where are the restrooms?	**Dove sono i gabinetti?** dō've sō'nō ō gäbēne'tē?
Can I do some laundry here?	**Si può lavare la propria biancheria qui?** sē pōō-ō' lävä're lä prō'prē-ä byänkerē'ä kōō-ē'?
Do you have any lockers?	**Ci sono delle cassette di sicurezza?** tshē sō'nō de'le käse'te dē sēkōōre'tsä?
When do I have to be back by?	**Fino a che ora si può rientrare la sera?** fē'nō ä ke ō'rä sē pōō-ō' rē-enträ're lä se'rä?
How can I get to the middle of town?	**Come si arriva in centro?** kō'me sē ärē'vä ēn tshen'trō?
Where's the nearest bus stop?	**Dov'è la fermata dell'autobus più vicina?** dōve' lä fermä'tä delou'tōbōōs pyōō vētshē'nä?

Camping

| May we camp on your property? | **Possiamo campeggiare sul vostro terreno?** pōsyä'mō kämpejä're sōōl vōs'trō tere'nō? |

47

Do you still have room for …?	**Ci sono ancora posti per …?** tshē sō'nō änkō'rä pō'stē per …?
What is the charge for …	**Quanto si paga per …** kōō·än'tō sē pä'gä per …
… adults and … children?	**… adulti e … bambini?** … ädōōl'tē e … bämbē'nē?
a car with a trailer?	**una macchina con roulotte?** ōō'nä mä'kēnä kōn rōōlōt'?
a camping van?	**un camper?** ōōn käm'per?
a tent?	**una tenda?** ōō'nä ten'dä?
Do you also rent *cabins/camping trailers?*	**Affittate anche *bungalows/roulotte?*** äfētä'te än'ke *bōōn'gälōs/rōōlōt'?*
We'd like a place in the shade.	**Vorremmo un posto all'ombra.** vōre'mō ōōn pō'stō älōm'brä.
We'd like to stay for one *night/… nights.*	**Vorremmo rimanere per *una notte/ … notti.*** vōre'mō rēmäne're per *ōō'nä nō'te/… nō'tē.*
Where can we *pitch our tent/park our van?*	**Dove possiamo *piantare la tenda/ parcheggiare la roulotte?*** dō've pōsyä'mō *pyäntä're lä ten'dä/pärkejä're lä rōōlōt'?*
Where are the bathrooms?	**Dove sono i bagni?** dō've sō'nō ē bä'nyē?

48

Where are the rest rooms?	**Dove sono i gabinetti?**
	dō've sō'nō ē gäbēne'tē?
Is there a power outlet here?	**C'è una presa di corrente qui?**
	tshe ōō'nä pre'sä dē kören'te kōō·ē'?
Where can I ...	**Dove si può ...** dō've sē pōō·ō' ...

empty the chemical waste from the toilet?
svuotare il WC chimico?
svōō-ōtä're ēl vōō-tshe' kē'mēkō?

empty sewage water?
versare l'acqua di scarico?
versä're lä'kōō·ä dē skä'rēko?

fill the tank with fresh water?
fare rifornimento di acqua?
fä're rēfōrnēmen'tō dē ä'kōō·ä?

Does the hot shower cost extra?	**Bisogna pagare extra per la doccia calda?** bēzō'nyä pägä're ek'strä per lä dō'tshä käl'dä?
Is there a grocery store here?	**C'è un negozio di alimentari qui?** tshe ōōn negō'tsyō dē älēmentä're kōō·ē'?
Can I *rent/exchange* gas cylinders here?	**Dove si *comprano/cambiano* le bombole del gas qui?** dō've sē *kōm'pränō/ käm'byänō* le bōm'bōle del gäs kōō·ē'?
May I borrow a(n) ..., please?	**Per favore, mi potrebbe prestare ...?** per fävō're, mē pōtre'be prestä're ...?

2

49

air mattress	**il materassino gonfiabile**
	ēl mäteräse'nō gönfyä'bēle
bathrooms	**i bagni** ē bä'nyē
bed linens	**la biancheria (da letto)**
	lä byänkerē'ä (dä le'tō)
breakfast	**la prima colazione** lä prē'mä kōlätsyō'ne
cabin	**il bungalow** ēl bōōn·gälō'
to camp, to go camping	**campeggiare** kämpejä're
camping	**il campeggio** ēl kämpe'jō
– permit	**la tessera di campeggio**
	lä te'serä dē kämpe'jō
– trailer	**la roulotte** lä rōōlōt'
– van	**il camper** ēl käm'per
campsite	**il campeggio** ēl kämpe'jō
candle	**la candela** lä kän'delä
check-in	**la registrazione** lä rejēsträtsyō'ne
chemical toilet *(in a van)*	**il WC chimico** ēl vōō-tshe' kē'mēkō
communal room	**la sala di soggiorno** lä sä'lä dē sōjōr'nō
to cook	**cucinare** kōōtshēnä're
detergent	**il detersivo** ēl detersē'vō
dining room	**la sala da pranzo** lä sä'lä dä prän'tsō
dinner	**la cena** lä tshe'nä
dormitory	**il dormitorio**
	ēl dōrmētōr'yō
double room	**la camera doppia** lä kä'merä dō'pyä

drier *(clothes)*	**l'asciugabiancheria** läshōōgäbyänkerĕ'ä
drinking water	**l'acqua potabile** lä'kōō-ä potä'bēle
electricity	**la corrente** lä kōren'te
to fill (up)	**riempire** rē-empē're
foam (insulation) mat	**la stuoia isolante** lä stōō-ō'yä ēsōlän'te
gas canister	**la cartuccia del gas** lä kärtōō'tshä del gäs
gas cylinder	**la bombola del gas** lä bōm'bōlä del gäs
gas lantern	**la lampada a gas** lä läm'pädä ä gäs
group of kids	**il gruppo giovanile** ēl grōō'pō jōvänĕ'le
hammer	**il martello** ēl märte'lō
hostel father	**il papà albergatore** ēl päpä' älbergätō're
hostel mother	**la mamma albergatrice** lä mä'mä älbergätrē'tshe
to iron	**stirare** stērä're
locker	**la cassetta di sicurezza** lä käse'tä dē sēkōōre'tsä
lunch	**il pranzo** ēl prän'tsō
membership card	**la tessera di membro** lä te'serä dē mem'brō
mosquito net	**la zanzariera** lä dzändzärēe'ra
mosquito repellant	**il fornellino antizanzare** ēl fōrnelē'nō äntēdzän'dzäre
outlet	**la presa di corrente** lä pre'sä dē kōren'te
overnight stay	**il pernottamento** ēl pernōtämen'tō
to set up	**piantare** pyäntä're
plates	**i piatti** ē pyä'tē

playground	**il campo da gioco** ēl käm'pō dä jō'kō
plug	**la spina** lä spē'nä
pot	**la pentola** lä pen'tōlä
to rent	**noleggiare** nōlejä're
rental fee	**la tariffa di noleggio** lä tärē'fä dē nōle'jō
room	**la camera** lä kä'merä
shower	**la doccia** lä dō'tshä
to take a shower	**fare la doccia** fä're lä dō'tshä
site	**il posto** ēl pō'stō
sleeping bag	**il sacco a pelo** ēl sä'kō ä pe'lō
stove *(camping)*	**il fornello** ēl fōrne'lō
tent	**la tenda** lä ten'dä
– peg	**il picchetto** ēl pēke'tō
toilet	**il gabinetto** ēl gäbēne'tō
usage fee	**la tariffa per l'uso** lä tärē'fä per lōō'zō
to wash	**lavare** lävä're
washing machine	**la lavatrice** lä lävätrē'tshe
water canister	**la tanica per l'acqua** lä tä'nēkä per lä'kōō·ä
youth hostel	**l'ostello della gioventù** lōste'lō de'lä jōventōō'
youth hostel card	**la tessera per gli ostelli della gioventù** lä te'serä per lyē ōste'lē de'lä jōventōō'

52

On the Way

ASKING THE WAY

Excuse me, where is …?	**Scusi, dov'è …?** skōō'zē, dōve' …

How can I get to …?	**Come si arriva a …?** kō'me sē ärē'vä ä …?

What's the *quickest/ cheapest* way to get to the …	**Come si arriva nel modo più** *veloce/ economico* … kō'me sē ärē'vä nel mō'dō pyōō velō'tshe/ekōnō'mēkō …

train station?	**alla stazione?** ä'lä stätsyō'ne?
bus station?	**alla stazione dei pullman?** ä'lä stätsyō'ne de'ē pōōl'män?
airport?	**all'aeroporto?** älä-erōpōr'tō?
harbor?	**al porto?** äl pōr'tō?

❗ **Il modo migliore è con il taxi.** • ēl mō'dō mēlyō're e kōn ēl tä'ksē.	The best thing to do is take a taxi.

How do I get to the interstate highway?	**Come si arriva all'autostrada?** kō'me sē ärē'vä äloutōsträ'dä?

❗ **Mi dispiace, non lo so.** • mē dēspyä'tshe, nōn lō sō.	I'm afraid I don't know.

❗ **Là.** lä.	Over there.

❗ **Indietro.** ēndye'trō.	Go back.

❗ **Sempre diritto.** sem'pre dērē'tō.	Straight ahead.

54

! A destra. ä de'strä. To the right.

! A sinistra. ä sēnē'strä. To the left.

! La _prima/seconda_ strada a _sinistra/destra_. lä prē'mä/sekōn'dä strä'dä ä sēnē'strä/de'strä. The _first/second_ street to the _left/ right_.

! Al semaforo. äl semä'fōrō. At the traffic lights.

• Dopo l'incrocio. dō'pō lēnkrō'tshō. After the intersection.

Attraversi ... äträver'sē ... Cross ...

! il ponte! ēl pōn'te. the bridge.
• la piazza! lä pyä'tsä. the square.
la strada! lä strä'dä. the street.

• Poi chieda a qualcun altro. poi kye'dä ä kōō·älkōōn' äl'trō. Then ask again.

Può prendere ... pōō·ō' pren'dere ... You can take ...

! l'autobus. lou'tōbōōs the bus.
• il tram. ēl träm. the streetcar.
la metropolitana. lä metrōpōlētä'nä the subway.

Is this the road to ...? **È questa la strada per ...?** e kōō·e'stä lä strä'dä per ...?

3

| How far is it? | **Quant'è lontano?** kōō·änte′ lōntä′nō? |

> **!** **Abbastanza lontano.**
> • äbästän′tsä lōntä′nō.
>
> Pretty far.

> **!** **Non è lontano.** nōn e lōntä′nō.
>
> Not (very) far.

> **!** **È qui vicino.** e kōō·ē vētshē′nō.
>
> It's very close.

| How many minutes on foot/by car? | **Quanti minuti ci vogliono *a piedi/con la macchina*?** kōō·än′tē mēnōō′tē tshē vō·lyō′nō *ä pye′dē/kōn lä mä/kēnä*? |

| Could you show me on the map? | **Me lo può indicare sulla cartina, per favore?** me lō pōō·ō′ ēndēkä′re sōō′lä kärtē′nä, per fävō′re? |

AT THE BORDER

Passport Control

> **!** **I (Suoi) documenti, per favore.**
> • ē (sōō·oi′) dōkōōmen′tē, per fävō′re.
>
> May I see your documents, please?

> **!** **Il Suo passaporto, per favore.**
> • ēl sōō′ō päsäpōr′tō, per fävō′re.
>
> May I see your passport, please?

> **!** **Il Suo passaporto è scaduto.**
> • ēl sōō′ō päsäpōr′tō e skädōō′tō.
>
> Your passport is expired.

56

I'm with the ... group.	**Faccio parte della comitiva ...** fä'tshō pär'te de'lä kōmētē'vä ...

Customs

? **Ha qualcosa da dichiarare?** ä kōō·älkō'sä dä dēkyärä're?

Do you have anything to declare?

! **Apra *il portabagagli/la valigia*, per favore.** ä'prä *ēl pōrtäbägä'lyē/ lä välē'jä*, per fävō're.

Open the *trunk/ suitcase*, please.

! **Deve sdoganare questo.** de've zdōgänä're kōō·e'stō.

You have to declare that.

At the Border

3

bill	**la fattura** lä fätōō'rä
border	**la frontiera** lä frōntye'rä
car registration	**i documenti dell'autoveicolo** e dōkōōmen'tē deloutōve·e'kōlō
country identi- fication sticker	**la targa di nazionalità** lä tär'gä dē nätsyōnälētä'
customs	**la dogana** lä dōgä'nä
– declaration	**la dichiarazione doganale** lä dēkyärätsyō'ne dōgänä'le
date	**la data** lä dä'tä
documents	**i documenti** e dōkōōmen'tē
driver's license	**la patente (di guida)** lä päten'te (de gōō·e'dä)
expired	**scaduto** skädōō'tō

57

first name	**il nome** ēl nō´me
identity	**la carta d'identità** lä kär´tä dēdentētä´
invalid	**non valido** nōn vä´lēdō
last name	**il cognome** ēl kōnyō´me
nationality	**la nazionalità** lä nätsyōnälētä´
passport	**il passaporto** ēl päsäpōr´tō
– control	**il controllo dei passaporti** ēl kōntrō´lō de´ē päsäpōr´tē
residence *(permanent)*	**la residenza** lä rezēden´tsä
residence *(temporary)*	**il domicilio** ēl dōmētshē´lyō
to renew	**prolungare** prōlōōn·gä´re
travel group	**la comitiva turistica** lä kōmētē´vä tōōrē´stēkä
VAT	**l'IVA (imposta sul valore aggiunto)** lēvä´ (ēmpō´stä sōōl väl´ōˑre äjōōn´tō)

LUGGAGE

May I *leave/pick up* my luggage here?	**Vorrei *depositare/ritirare* i miei bagagli.** vōre'ē dēpōsētä're/rētērä're ē mye'ē bägä'lyē.
May I leave my backpack with you *for an hour/until* …?	**Potrei lasciare qui il mio zaino *per un'ora/fino a* …?** pōtre'ē läshä're kōō-ē' ēl mē'ō dzī'nō per ōōnō'rä/fē'nō ä …?
I'd like to have these bags sent to …	**Vorrei spedire questo bagaglio per …** vōre'ē spedē're kōō-e'stō bägä'lyō per …
When will they be at …?	**Quando arriverà a … ?** kōō-än'dō ärēverä' ä …?
My luggage hasn't arrived (yet).	**I miei bagagli non sono (ancora) arrivati.** ē mye'ē bägä'lyē nōn sō'nō (änkō'rä) ärēvä'tē.
Where is my luggage?	**Dove sono i miei bagagli?** dō've sō'nō ē mye'ē bägä'lyē?
Those aren't my things.	**Queste non sono le mie cose.** kōō-e'ste nōn sō'nō le mē'e kō'se.
A suitcase is missing.	**Manca una valigia.** män'kä ōō'nä välē'jä.
My luggage has been damaged.	**La mia valigia è stata danneggiata.** lä mē'ä välē'jä e stä'ta danejä'tä.
Who can I report it to?	**A chi mi posso rivolgere?** ä kē mē pō'sō rēvōl'jere?

3

59

backpack	**lo zaino** lō dzī´nō
bag	**la borsa** lä bôr´sä
baggage	**il bagaglio** ēl bägä´lyō
– check-in	**l'accettazione** *f* **bagagli** lätshetätsyō´ne bägä´lyē
– claim	**la riconsegna bagagli** lä rēkōnse´nyä bägä´lyē
– storage	**il deposito bagagli** ēl depō´sētō bägä´lyē
– ticket	**lo scontrino dei bagagli** lō skōntrē´nō de´ē bägä´lyē
carry-on baggage	**il bagaglio a mano** ēl bägä´lyō ä mä´nō
to check in *(baggage)*	**depositare** depōsētä´re
excess baggage	**l'eccesso di bagaglio** letshe´sō dē bägä´lyo
flight bag	**la borsa da viaggio** lä bôr´sä dä vyä´jō
to leave here	**lasciare qui** läshä´re kōō-ē´
locker	**il deposito bagagli a cassette** ēl depō´sētō bägä´lyē ä käse´te
to pick up	**ritirare** rētērä´re
suitcase	**la valigia** lä välē´jä

PLANE

Information and Booking

Where is the ... counter?	**Dov'è lo sportello della ...?** dōve' lō spōrte'lō de'lä ...?
When is the next flight to ...?	**Quando parte il prossimo aereo per ...?** kōō·än'dō pär'te ĕl prō'sēmō ä·e're·ō per ...?
When will a plane be flying to ... *today/tomorrow*?	**Quando parte *oggi/domani* un aereo per ...?** kōō·än'dō pär'te ō'jē/dōmä'nē ōōn ä·e're·ō per ...?
When will we be in ...?	**Quando arriviamo a ...?** kōō·än'dō ärēvyä'mō ä ...?
How much will it cost to fly to ... (round-trip)?	**Quanto costa un volo (di andata e ritorno) per ...?** kōō·än'tō kō'stä ōōn vō'lō (dē ändä'tä e rētōr'nō) per ...?
I'd like a ... ticket to ..., please.	**Un biglietto per ..., per favore, ...** ōōn bēlye'tō per ..., per fävō're.
one-way.	**di sola andata.** dē sō'lä ändä'tä.
round-trip.	**di andata e ritorno.** dē ändä'tä e rētōr'nō.
economy class.	**di classe turistica.** dē klä'se tōōrē'stēkä.
business class.	**di business class.** dē bēz'nes kläs.
first-class.	**di prima classe.** dē prē'mä klä'se.

3

61

Purtroppo su questo volo non ci sono più posti. pŏŏrtrŏ′pō sōō kōō-e′stō vō′lō nōn tshē sō′nō pyōō pō′stē.

I'm afraid this flight is booked out.

Are there any *special rates/stand-by seats* available?	**Ci sono *tariffe speciali/posti stand-by*?** tshē sō′nō tärē′fe spetsh-ä′lē/pō′stē ständ′bī?
I'd like …	**Vorrei un posto …** vōre′ē ōōn pō′stō …
a window seat.	**accanto al finestrino.** äkän′tō äl fēnestrē′nō.
an aisle seat.	**accanto al corridoio.** äkän′tō äl kōrēdoi′ō.
a seat in non-smoking.	**per non fumatori.** per nōn fōōmätō′rē.
a seat in smoking.	**per fumatori.** per fōōmätō′rē.
Where is Gate B?	**Dov'è l'uscita B?** dōve′ lōōshē′tä bē?
How late is the flight to … ?	**Quanto ritardo ha l'aereo per …?** kōō-än′tō rētär′dō ä lä-e′re-ō per …?
I'd like to *confirm/cancel* my flight.	**Vorrei *confermare/annullare* questo volo.** vōre′ē kōnfermä′re/änōōlä′re kōō-e′stō vō′lō.
I'd like to change my flight.	**Vorrei cambiare la data del biglietto.** vōre′ē kämbyä′re lä dä′tä del bēlye′tō.

On the Plane

Could I have *(another/some more)* …, please?	**Per favore, potrei avere (ancora) … ?** per fävö're, pōtre'ē äve're (änkō'rä) …?
I feel sick.	**Mi sento male.** mē sen'tō mä'le.
When do we land?	**Quando atterriamo?** kōō·än'dō äteryä'mō?

Plane

airline	**la compagnia aerea** lä kōmpänyē'ä ä·e're·ä
airplane	**l'aereo** lä·e're·ō
airport	**l'aeroporto** lä·erōpōr'tō
– tax	**la tassa aeroportuale** lä tä'sä ä·erōpōrtōō·ä'le
airsickness	**il mal d'aria** ēl mäl d'ä'ryä
arrival	**l'arrivo** lärē'vō
to book	**prenotare** prenōtä're
to cancel	**annullare** änōōlä're
to change a flight	**cambiare la data del biglietto** kämbyä're lä dä'tä del bēlye'tō
charter flight	**il volo charter** ēl vō'lō tshär'ter
class	**la classe** lä klä'se
to confirm	**confermare** kōnfermä're
counter	**lo sportello** lō spōrte'lō
delay	**il ritardo** ēl rētär'dō
departure	**il decollo** ēl dekō'lō

3

exit	**l'uscita** lōōshē'tä
flight	**il volo** ēl vō'lō
– attendant *(female)*	**l'hostess** *f* lŏs'tes
– attendant *(male)*	**lo steward** *m* lō styōō'ärd
return –	**il volo di ritorno** ēl vō'lō dē rētōr'nō
scheduled –	**il volo di linea** ēl vō'lō dē lē'ne-ä
to fly	**andare in aereo** ändä're ēn ä-e're-ō
hand baggage	**il bagaglio a mano** ēl bägä'lyō ä mä'nō
information desk	**l'ufficio informazioni** lōōfē'tshō ēnfōrmätsyō'nē
to land	**atterrare** äterä're
local time	**l'ora locale** lō'rä lōkä'le
nonsmoker	**non fumatori** *m/pl* nōn fōōmätō'rē
smoker	**fumatori** *m/pl* fōōmätō'rē
stopover	**lo scalo** lō skä'lō
to take off	**decollare** dekōlä're
ticket	**il biglietto** ēl bēlye'tō

RAIL

Information and Tickets

Where is the *train/ tourist* information office?	**Dov'è l'ufficio *informazioni/turistico*?** dōve' lōōfē'tshō ēnfōrmätsyō'nē/ tōōrē'stēkō?
Where can I find the *baggage storage/ lockers*?	**Dov'è il *deposito bagagli/deposito bagagli a cassette*?** dōve' ēl depō'sētō bägä'lyē/depō'sētō bägä'lyē ä käse'te?

INFO It is more common to travel by train in Italy than in the United States. A normal second-class ticket does not include a seat reservation; you may choose from whichever seats are not taken. You have a choice of trains between the **rapidi** rä'pēdē (express trains that stop only at cities) and the **espressi** espre'sē (local trains that stop more frequently). Recently a third option has been added: the **treni ad alta velocità** tre'nē äd äl'tä velōtshētä' (high-speed trains), for which you must pay extra and are required to reserve a seat. Some of these trains only have first-class cars. No matter which train you take, it would be a good idea to reserve a seat since the trains are often very full. You can make your reservations up to an hour before departure.

When is the *next/last* train to …?	**Quando parte il prossimo/l'ultimo treno per …?** kōō·än'dō pär'te el prō'sēmō/lōōl'tēmō tre'nō per …?
When will it arrive in …?	**Quando arriva a …?** kōō·än'dō ärē'vä ä …?
When are the trains to …?	**Che treni ci sono per …?** ke tre'nē tshē sō'nō per …?
Do I have to change trains?	**Devo cambiare?** de'vō kämbyä're?
Which platform does the train to … leave from?	**Da quale binario parte il treno per …?** dä kōō·ä'le bēnär'yō pär'te el tre'nō per …?

How much does a ticket to … cost?	**Quanto costa il biglietto per … ?** kōō-än'tō kō'stä ēl bēlye'tō per … ?
Are there special rates for …?	**C'è una riduzione per …?** tshe ōō'nä rēdōōtsēō'ne per … ?
Do you have to pay extra for this train?	**Per questo treno ci vuole il supplemento?** per kōō-e'stō tre'nō tshē vōō-o'le ēl sōōplemen'tō?
I'd like a … ticket/ two … tickets to …, please.	**Un biglietto/Due biglietti per …, per favore, …** ōōn bēlye'tō/dōō'e bēlye'tē per …, per fävō're, …
one-way	**di sola andata.** dē sō'lä ändä'tä.
round-trip	**di andata e ritorno.** dē ändä'tä e rētōr'nō.
first/second class	**di prima/seconda classe.** dē prē'mä/sekōn'dä klä'se.
for children.	**per bambini.** per bämbē'nē.

INFO If you have a round-trip ticket, you must get it stamped before you begin the return portion of your trip. There are special machines at the train station for this purpose.

I'd like to reserve a seat on the … o'clock train to …, please.	**Vorrei prenotare un posto sul treno delle … per …, per favore.** vōre'ē prenōtä're ōōn pō'stō sōōl tre'nō de'le … per …, per fävō're.

I'd like a seat …	**Vorrei un posto …** vōre'ē ōōn pō'stō …
by the window.	**accanto al finestrino.**
	äkän'tō äl fēnestrē'nō.
in nonsmoking.	**per non fumatori.**
	per nōn fōōmätō'rē.
in smoking.	**per fumatori.** per fōōmätō'rē.
I'd like to bring a bicycle with me.	**Vorrei portarmi dietro la bicicletta.**
	vōre'ē pōrtär'mē dye'trō lä bētshēkle'tä.

Information

Accettazione bagagli ätshetätsyō'ne bägä'lyē	Baggage Check-In
Ai binari ī bēnä'rē	To All Trains
Binario bēnär'yō	Track
Deposito bagagli depō'sēto bägä'lyē	Baggage Storage
Deposito bagagli a cassette depō'sēto bägä'lyē ä käse'te	Lockers
Gabinetti gäbēne'tē	Rest Rooms
Informazioni ēnfōrmätsyō'nē	Information
Ristorante rēstōrän'te	Restaurant
Sala d'aspetto sä'lä däspe'tō	Waiting Room
Uscita ōōshē'tä	Exit

3

On the Train

May I sit here?	**È libero questo posto?** e lē'berō kōō·e'stō pō'stō?
Excuse me, but I believe this is my seat.	**Scusi, ma questo è il mio posto.** skōō'zē, mä kōō·e'stō e ēl mē'ō pō'stō.
Would you mind if I *opened/closed* the window?	**Posso *aprire/chiudere* il finestrino?** pō'sō *äprē're/kyōō'dere* ēl fēnestrē'nō?

! **I biglietti, prego!** ē bēlye'tē, pre'gō! Tickets, please!

How many more stops to …?	**Quante stazioni ci sono ancora prima di … ?** kōō·än'te stätsyō'nē tshē sō'nō änkō'rä prē'mä dē …?
How long is our layover?	**Quanto tempo si ferma il treno?** kōō·än'tō tem'pō sē fer'mä ēl tre'nō?
Will I be in time to catch the train to …?	**Faccio ancora in tempo a prendere il treno per … ?** fä'tshō änkō'rä ēn tem'pō ä pren'dere ēl tre'nō per …?

Train

to arrive	**arrivare**	ärēvä're
car	**il vagone**	ēl vägō'ne
to change (trains)	**cambiare**	kämbyä're
class	**la classe**	lä klä'se
compartment	**lo scompartimento**	lō skōmpärtēmen'tō
connection	**la coincidenza**	lä kō·ēntshēden'tsä

to depart	**partire** pärtē're
dining car	**il vagone ristorante**
	ēl vägō'ne rēstōrän'te
discount	**la riduzione** lä rēdōōtsyō'ne
exit	**l'uscita** lōōshē'tä
extra cost	**il supplemento** ēl sōōplemen'tō
to get off	**scendere** shen'dere
to get on	**salire** sälē're
to go by train	**andare in treno** ändä're ēn tre'nō
fare	**il prezzo del biglietto**
	ēl pre'tsō del bēlye'tō
lockers	**il deposito bagagli a cassette**
	ēl depō'sētō bägä'lyē ä käse'te
platform	**il binario** ēl bēnär'yō
reserved	**prenotato** prenōtä'tō
seat	**il posto** ēl pō'stō
sleeping car	**il vagone letto** ēl vägō'ne le'tō
(1–4 beds)	
sleeping car	**la carrozza con cuccette**
(many beds)	lä kärō'tsä kōn kōōtshe'te
stop	**la fermata** lä fermä'tä
occupied	**occupato** ōkōōpä'tō
through car	**la carrozza diretta** lä kärō'tsä dēre'tä
ticket	**il biglietto** ēl bēlye'tō
timetable	**l'orario** lōrär'yō
track	**il binario** ēl bēnär'yō
train	**il treno** ēl tre'nō
– station	**la stazione** lä stätsyō'ne

3

69

BOAT

Information and Booking

When will there be a *ship*/*ferry* going to ...?	**Quando parte *una nave*/*un traghetto* per ...?** kōō·än′dō pär′te ōō′nä nä′ve/ ōōn träge′tō per ...)
How long is the passage to ...?	**Quanto dura la traversata fino a ... ?** kōō·än′tō dōō′rä lä träversä′tä fē′nō ä ...?
At which *ports*/*islands* will we be landing?	**Quali *porti*/*isole* si toccano?** kōō·ä′lē pōr′tē/ē′zōle sē tōkä′nō?
When do we land?	**Quando sbarchiamo a ... ?** kōō·än′dō zbärkyä′mō ä ...?
When must we be on board?	**Quando dobbiamo essere a bordo?** kōō·än′dō dōbyä′mō e′sere ä bōr′dō?
I'd like to board with a car.	**Vorrei imbarcare la macchina.** vōre′ē ēmbärkä′re lä mä′kēnä.
I'd like a *first class*/*tourist class* ticket to ...	**Vorrei un biglietto di *prima classe*/ *classe turistica* per ...** vōre′ē ōōn bēlye′tō dē prē′mä klä′se/klä′se tōōrē′stēkä per ...
I'd like a single cabin.	**Vorrei una cabina singola.** vōre′ē ōō′nä käbē′nä sēn′gōlä.
I'd like a ticket for the excursion at ... o'clock.	**Vorrei un biglietto per il giro delle ...** vōre′ē ōōn bēlye′tō per ēl jē′rō de′le ...

70

| Where has the ... docked? | **Dov'è approdata la ... ?**
dōve' äprŏdä'tä lä ...? |
| | |

On Board

I'm looking for cabin number ...	**Cerco la cabina numero ...** tsher'ko lä kä'bēnä nōō'merō ...
May I have a different cabin?	**Potrei avere un'altra cabina?** pōtre'ē äve're ōōnäl'trä käbē'nä?
Do you have something for seasickness?	**Ha qualcosa contro il mal di mare?** ä kōō·äl'kō'sa kōn'trō ēl mäl dē mä're?

Boat

air conditioning	**l'impianto dell'aria condizionata** lēmpyän'tō delär'yä kōndētsyōnä'tä
blanket	**la coperta di lana** lä kōper'tä dē lä'nä
boat trip	**la crociera** lä krŏtshe'rä
cabin	**la cabina** lä käbē'nä
double –	**la cabina doppia** lä käbē'nä dō'pyä
exterior –	**la cabina esterna** lä käbē'nä ester'nä
four-bed –	**la cabina a quattro posti** lä käbē'nä ä kōō·ä'trō pō'stē
interior –	**la cabina interna** lä käbē'nä ēnter'nä
single –	**la cabina singola** lä käbē'nä sēn'gōlä
canal	**il canale** ēl känä'lo
captain	**il capitano** ēl käpētä'nō
car ferry	**la nave traghetto** lä nä've träge'to
coast	**la costa** lä kō'stä

3

71

deck	**la coperta**	lä kōper'tä
duty	**i diritti portuali**	ē dērē'tē pōrtōō-ä'lē
duty-free store	**il duty-free-shop**	ēl dēōō'tē-frē-shōp'
excursion	**la gita**	lä jē'tä
ferry	**il traghetto**	ēl träge'tō
hovercraft	**l'hoverkraft** *m*	lō'verkräft
island	**l'isola**	lē'zōlä
land excursion	**la gita a terra**	lä jē'tä ä te'rä
landing	**l'approdo**	läprō'dō
life boat	**la scialuppa di salvataggio**	
		lä shälōō'pä dē sälvätä'jō
life vest	**il giubbotto di salvataggio**	
		ēl jōōbō'tō dē sälvätä'jō
lounge chair	**la sedia a sdraio**	lä se'dyä ä zdrī'ō
passage	**la traversata**	lä träversä'tä
port *(harbor)*	**il porto**	ēl pōr'tō
port *(side of boat)*	**a babordo**	ä bäbōr'dō
rough sea	**il mare mosso**	ēl mä're mō'sō
sea	**il mare**	ēl mä're
– sickness	**il mal di mare**	ēl mäl dē mä're
ship	**la nave**	lä nä've
ship's agent	**l'agenzia navale**	läjen'tsyä nävä'le
shore	**la riva**	lä rē'vä
starboard	**a dritta**	ä drē'tä
steward	**il cameriere**	ēl kämerye're
sun deck	**il ponte di passeggiata**	
		ēl pōn'te dē päsejä'tä
swimming pool	**la piscina**	lä pēshē'nä

CAR, MOTORBIKE AND BIKE

Rentals

I'd like to rent a … (with automatic transmission).	**Vorrei noleggiare … (con il cambio automatico).** vōre′ē nōlejä′re … (kōn ēl käm′byō outōmä′tēkō).
car	**una macchina** ōō′nä mä′kenä
car with four-wheel drive	**un fuoristrada** ōōn fōō-ōrēsträ′dä
motorcycle	**una motocicletta** ōō′nä mōtōtshēkle′tä
motor home	**un camper** ōōn käm′per

? **Mi fa vedere la Sua patente, per favore?** mē fä vede′re lä sōō′ä pätėn′te, per fävō′re? | May I see your driver's license, please? | **3** |

I'd like to rent a *bicycle/mountain bike* (with back-pedal brakes).	**Vorrei noleggiare una *bicicletta/mountain bike* … con il freno a contropedale.** vōre′ē nōlejä′re ōō′nä bētshēkle′tä/moun′ten bīk (kōn ēl fre′nō ä kōntrōpedä′le).
I'd like to rent it (for) …	**La vorrei noleggiare per …** lä vōre′ē nōlejä′re per …
tomorrow.	**domani.** dōmä′nē.
one day.	**un giorno.** ōōn jōr′nō.
two days.	**due giorni.** dōō′e jōr′nē.
one week.	**una settimana.** ōō′nä setēmä′nä.

? **Che tipo di macchina vuole?**
ke tē'pō dē mä'kēnä vōō-ō'le?

What kind of car
would you like?

How much will that cost?	**Quanto costa?** kōō·än'tō kō'stä?
How much mileage is included in the price?	**Quanti chilometri sono compresi nel prezzo?** kōō·än'tē kēlō'metrē sō'nō kômpre'sē nel pre'tsō?
What kind of fuel does it take?	**Che tipo di carburante ci vuole?** ke tē'pō dē kärbōorän'te tshe vōō·ō'le?
Is comprehensive insurance included?	**È inclusa un'assicurazione a copertura totale?** e ēnklōō'zä ōōnäsēkōōrätsyō'ne ä kōpertōō'rä tōtä'le?
What's the deductible?	**A quanto ammonta la quota a carico del cliente?** ä kōō·än'tō ämōn'tä lä kōō·ō'tä ä kä'rēkō del klē·en'te?
Can I return the car in …?	**Posso riconsegnare la macchina anche a … ?** pō'sō rēkōnsenyä're lä mä'kēnä än'ke ä …?

INFO Roads in Italy fall into various categories. When driving on the **strada communale,** the **strada provinciale** strä'dä kōmōōnä'le, strä'dä prōventshä'le (state road), or the **strada statale** strä'dä stätä'le (interstate road), you must honor the 90 km/h (app. 55 mph) speed limit. You may drive up to 110 km/h (app. 65 mph) on the **superstrada** sōōpersträ'dä (interstate highway) and up to 130 km/h (app. 75 mph) on the **autostrada** outōsträ'dä (national highway).

74

When do I have to be back?	**Quando devo essere di ritorno?**
	kōō·än'dō de'vō e'sere dē rētōr'nō?
I'd also like a helmet.	**Mi dia anche un casco, per favore.**
	mē dyä än'ke ōōn käs'kō, per fävō're.

Parking

Is there a *parking garage/parking lot* nearby?	**C'è un *garage/parcheggio* qui vicino?**
	tshe ōōn *gäräj'/pärke'jō* kōō·e' vētshē'no?
Is the parking lot supervised?	**Il parcheggio è custodito?**
	el pärke'jō e kōōstōdē'tō?
Do you pay at the exit or in advance?	**Si paga all' uscita, o devo pagare in anticipo?**
	sē pä'gä älōōshē'tä, ō de'vō pägä're ēn äntē'tshēpō?

INFO You must pay to park in spaces marked in blue, usually by getting a receipt from a ticket machine. Parking spaces marked in white are free.

Is the parking garage open all night?	**Il garage rimane aperto tutta la notte?**
	el gäräj' rēmä'ne äper'tō tōō'tä lä nō'te?
Can I park here?	**Posso parcheggiare qui?**
	pō'sō pärkejä're kōō·ē?

75

Where is/How far is it to the nearest gas station?	***Dov'è/Quant'è lontano il prossimo distributore?*** dōvĕ'/kōō-ănte' lōntä'nō ĕl prō'sēmō dēstrēbōōtō're?

INFO In Italy gas stations have the same opening hours as the stores. You will receive service during the working day. Many gas stations offer self-service at night or on Sundays: you must pay in advance at a machine for the amount of gas you need before filling your tank.

Fill it up, please.	**Il pieno, per favore!** ĕl pye'nō, per fävō're!
... euros' worth of ..., please.	**... euro di ..., per favore.** ... e'ōōrō dē ..., per fävōō're.
unleaded	**normale senza piombo** nōrmä'le sen'tsä pyōm'bō
diesel	**diesel** dē'sel
leaded	**normale** nōrmä'le
super unleaded	**super senza piombo** sōō'per sen'tsä pyōm'bō
super leaded	**super** sōō'per
two-stroke engine fuel	**miscela** mēshe'lä
Can I pay with this credit card?	**Posso pagare con questa carta di credito?** pō'sō pägä're kōn kōō-e'stä kär'tä dē kre'dētō?

I'd like *1 liter/2 liters* of oil, please.	**Vorrei *un litro/due litri* d'olio.**
	vôre'ē *ōōn lē'trō/dōō'e* lē'trē dō'lyō.
Could you change the oil, please?	**Cambi l'olio, per favore.**
	käm'bē lō'lyō, per fävō're.
I need snow chains.	**Mi servono delle catene da neve.**
	mē servō'nō de'le Kāte'ne dä ne've.

INFO The **autostrada** outōsträ'dä is a toll road in Italy. You must take a card from a machine at the toll area before you can drive onto the **autostrada**. When you drive off, you must pay the amount indicated on the card for the distance (in kilometers) you have driven.

Breakdown and Accidents

3

Please call ..., quickly!	**Presto, chiami ...** pre'stō, kyä'mē ...
an ambulance	**un'ambulanza!** ōōnämbōōlän'tsä!
the police	**la polizia!** lä pōlē'tsyä!
the fire department	**i vigili del fuoco!** ē vē'jēlē del fōō-ō-kō!
I've had an accident.	**Ho avuto un incidente.**
	ō ävōō'tō ōōn ēntshēden'te.
May I use your phone?	**Posso usare il Suo telefono?**
	pō'sō ōōzä're ēl sōō'ō tcle'fōnō?
Nobody's hurt.	**Non ci sono feriti.** nōn tshē sō'nō ferē'tē.

77

... people have been (seriously) injured.	**... persone sono rimaste (gravemente) ferite.** ... persŏ'ne sŏ'nŏ rĕmä'ste (grävemen'te) fĕrē'te.
Please help me.	**Mi aiuti, per favore!** mē äyōō'tĕ, per fävŏ're!
I need a first-aid kit.	**Mi servono bende, garza e cerotti.** mē servŏ'nŏ ben'de, gär'tsä e tsherŏ'tĕ.
I'm out of gas.	**Non ho più benzina.** nŏn ŏ pyŏŏ bentsē'nä.
Could you ...	**Potrebbe ...** pŏtrĕ'be ...
give me a lift?	**darmi un passaggio?** där'mē ōōn päsä'jŏ?
tow my car?	**rimorchiare la mia macchina?** rĕmŏrkyä're lä mē'ä mä'kēnä?
send me a tow-truck?	**mandarmi un carro attrezzi?** mändär'mē ōōn kä'rō ätre'tsē?
It's not my fault.	**Non è colpa mia.** nŏn e kŏl'pä mē'ä.
It's your fault.	**E' colpa Sua.** e kŏl'pä sōō'ä.
You didn't have the right-of-way.	**Lei non ha rispettato la precedenza.** le'ē nŏn ä rĕspetä'tŏ lä pretsheden'tsä.
I had the right of way.	**Avevo la precedenza.** äve'vŏ lä pretsheden'tsä.
You cut the corner.	**Lei ha tagliato la curva.** le'ē ä tälyä'tŏ lä kōōr'vä.

You were following too closely.	**Lei non ha rispettato la distanza regolamentare.** le'ē nôn ä rēspetä'tô lä dēstän'tsä regōlämentä're.
You were going too fast.	**Lei andava troppo forte.** le'ē ändä'vä trô'pô fôr'te.
I was doing … kilometers an hour.	**Andavo a … chilometri all'ora.** ändä'vô ä … kēlō'metrē älô'rä.
You damaged the …	**Ha danneggiato …** ä dänejä'tô …
May I have your *name and address/ insurance information*, please?	**Mi dia *il Suo nome e il Suo indirizzo/ il nome della Sua assicurazione*, per favore.** mē dē'ä *ēl sōō'ō nō'me e ēl sōō'ō ēndērē'tsō/ēl nō'me de'lä sōō'ä äsēkōōrätsyō'ne*, per fävō're.
Would you mind being a witness?	**Potrebbe testimoniare sull'accaduto?** pōtre'be testēmōnyä're sōōläkädoo'tô?
Thank you very much for your help.	**Grazie dell'aiuto.** grä'tsē·e deläyōō'tô.

! **I Suoi documenti, per favore.**
● ē sōō·oi' dōkōōmen'tē, per fävō're.

Your driver's license, registration, and insurance information, please.

! ***La Sua patente/Il Suo libretto de circolazione*, per favore!**
● lä sōō'ä päten'te/ēl sōō'ō lēbre'tô de tshērkolätsēō'ne, per fävō're!

Your *driver's licence/ registration*, please.

3

79

Could you lend me ..., please?	**Per favore, mi potrebbe prestare ...?**
	per fävō're, mē pōtre'be prestä're ...?
I need ...	**Mi servirebbe ...** mē servēre'be ...

a bicycle repair kit.	**il corredo per la riparazione di forature.** ēl kōre'do per lä rēpärätsyō'ne dē fōrätōō're.
a pump.	**una pompa dell'aria.** ōō'nä pōm'pä delär'yä.
a (...) wrench.	**una chiave inglese (da ...).** ōō'nä kyä've ēn·gle'se (dä ...).
a screwdriver.	**un cacciavite.** ōōn kätshäve'te.
a (...) socket wrench.	**una chiave fissa a tubo (da ...).** ōō'nä kyä've fē'sä ä tōō'bō (dä ...).
a jack.	**un cric.** ōōn krēk.
a tool kit.	**una scatola degli attrezzi.** ōō'nä skä'tōlä de'lyē ätre'tsē.
a pair of pliers.	**una tenaglia.** ōō'nä tenä'lyä.

At the Repair Shop

Where is the nearest (…) garage?	**Dov'è l'officina (concessionaria) più vicina?** dōve' lōfētshē'nä (kōntshesyōnär'yä) pyōō vētshē'nä?
My car's on the road to …	**La mia macchina sta sulla strada per …** lä mē'ä mä'kēnä sta (sōō'lä strä'dä per) …
Can you tow it away?	**La potete rimorchiare?** lä pōte'te rēmōrkyä're?
Would you have a look at it?	**Può dare un'occhiata?** pōō-ō' dä're ōōnōkyä'tä?
… is broken.	**… non funziona.** … non fōōntsyō'nä.
My car won't start.	**La mia macchina non parte.** lä mē'ä mä'kēnä nōn pär'te.
The battery is dead.	**La batteria è scarica.** lä bätere'ä e skä'rēkä.
The engine *sounds funny/doesn't have any power*.	**Il motore *fa dei rumori strani/non tira*.** ēl mōtō're *fä de'ē rōōmō'rē strä'nē/nōn tē'rä*.
Do you have the (original) parts for …	**Ha pezzi di ricambio (originali) per … ?** ä pe'tse dē rēkäm'byō (ōrējēnä'lē) per …?

3

81

Just do the essential repairs, please.	**Faccia soltanto le riparazioni più necessarie, per favore.** fä'shä sôltän'tō le rēpärätsyō'nē pyōō netshesär'ye, per fävö're.
When will it be ready?	**Per quando sarà pronta?** per kōō·än'dō särä' prōn'tä?
Can I still drive it?	**Posso ancora andarci in giro?** pō'sō änkō'rä ändär'tshē ēn jē'ro?

Car, Motorbike and Bike

to accelerate	**accelerare** ätshelerä're
accident	**l'incidente** *m* lēntshēden'te
air filter	**il filtro dell'aria** ēl fēl'trō delär'yä
antifreeze	**l'antigelo** läntēje'lō
automatic transmission	**il cambio automatico** ēl käm'byō outomä'tēko
battery	**la batteria** lä bäterē'ä
bicycle	**la bicicletta** lä bētshēkle'tä
brake	**il freno** ēl fre'nō
– fluid	**l'olio dei freni** lō'lyō de'ē fre'nē
– lights	**le luci d'arresto** le lōō'tshē däre'stō
bright lights	**il faro abbagliante** ēl fä'rō äbälyän'te
broken	**rotto** rō'tō
bulb	**la lampadina** lä lämpädē'nä
bumper	**il paraurti** ēl pärä-ōōr'tē
car	**la macchina** lä mä'kēnä
carburetor	**il carburatore** ēl kärbōōrätō're

82

catalytic converter	**la marmitta catalitica** lä märmë'tä kätälë'tēkä
to change	**cambiare** kämbyä're
child seat	**il seggiolino per l'auto** ēl sejōlë'nō per lou'tō
clutch	**la frizione** lä frētsyō'ne
state road	**la strada provinciale** lä strä'dä prōvēntshä'le
curve	**la curva** lä kōōr'vä
to drive	**andare (in macchina)** ändä're (ēn mä'kēnä)
driver's license	**la patente** lä päten'te
dynamo	**la dinamo** lä dē'nämō
emergency brake	**il freno a mano** ēl fre'nō ä mä'nō
engine	**il motore** ēl mōtō're
exhaust	**lo scappamento** lō skäpämen'tō
fan belt	**la cinghia** lä tshēn'gē·ä
fender	**il parafango** ēl päräfän'gō
first-aid kit	**la cassetta di pronto soccorso** lä käse'tä dē prōn'tō sōkōr'sō
four-wheel drive car	**il fuoristrada** ēl fōō·ōrēsträ'dä
fuse	**il fusibile** ēl fōōzē'bēle
garage	**l'officina** lōfētshē'nä
gas *(liquid fuel)*	**la benzina** lä bentsē'nä
gas *(gaseous fuel)*	**il gas** ēl gäs
– station	**il distributore** ēl dēstrēbōōtō're
gear	**la marcia** lä mär'tshä
headlights	**il faro** ēl fä'rō

3

83

helmet	**il casco** ēl käs'kō
highway	**l'autostrada** loutōsträ'dä
horn	**il clacson** ēl kläk'sōn
ignition	**l'accensione** *f* lätshensyō'ne
injured	**ferito** ferē'tō
innertube	**la camera d'aria** lä kä'merä där'yä
insurance	**l'assicurazione** *f* läsēkōōrätsyō'ne
international car	**il carnet di assistenza internazionale**
insurance	ēl kärne' dē äsēsten'tsä enternätsyönä'le
verification	
interstate road	**la (strada) statale** lä (strä'dä) stätä'le
joint	**la guarnizione** lä gōō-ärnētsyō'ne
kilometer	**il chilometro** ēl kēlō'metrō
light	**la luce** lä lōō'tshe
low beams	**il faro anabbagliante**
	ēl fä'rō änäbälyän'te
mirror	**lo specchio** lō spe'kyō
motorcycle	**la motocicletta** lä mōtōtshēkle'tä
neutral	**la marcia in folle** lä mär'tshä ēn fō'le
no parking	**il divieto di parcheggio**
	ēl dēvye'tō dē pärke'jō
oil	**l'olio del motore** lō'lyō del mōtō're
– change	**il cambio dell'olio**
	ēl käm'byō delō'lyō
to park	**parcheggiare** pärkejä're
parking garage	**il garage** ēl gäräj'
parking light	**le luci di posizione**
	le lōō'tshe dē pōzētsyō'ne
parking lot	**il parcheggio** ēl pärke'jō

parking meter	**il parchimetro**	ēl pärkē'metrō
parking receipt machine	**il distributore automatico di biglietti per il parcheggio**	ēl dēstrēbōōtō're outōmä'tēkō dē bēlye'tē per ēl pärke'jō
to put into gear	**innestare la marcia**	ēnestä're lä mär'tshä
radiator	**il radiatore**	ēl rädyätō're
rear-end collision	**il tamponamento**	ēl tämpōnämen'tō
registration number	**il numero di targa**	ēl nōō'merō dē tär'gä
to rent	**noleggiare**	nōlejä're
to repair	**riparare**	rēpärä're
seatbelt	**la cintura di sicurezza**	lä tshintōō'rä dē sēkōōre'tsä
shock absorber	**l'ammortizzatore** *m*	lämörtētsätō're
snow chains	**le catene da neve**	le käte'ne dä ne've
spare gas canister	**la tanica di riserva**	lä tä'nēkä dē rēzer'vä
spare part	**il pezzo di ricambio**	ēl pe'tsō dē rēkäm'byō
spare tire	**la ruota di scorta**	lä rōō-ō'tä dē skōr'tä
spark plug	**la candela d'accensione**	lä kände'lä dätshensyō'ne
starter	**lo starter**	lō stär'ter
steering	**lo sterzo**	lō ster'tso
tail light	**il fanalino posteriore**	ēl fänälē'nō pōsteryō're
tire	**la ruota**	lä rōō-ō'tä

toll	**il pedaggio** ēl pedä'jō
– booth	**il casello autostradale**
	ēl käse'lō outōsträdä'le
– road	**il tratto stradale soggetto a pedaggio**
	ēl trä'tō strädä'le sōje'tō ä pedä'jō
to tow (away)	**rimorchiare** rēmōrkyä're
tow rope	**il cavo da rimorchio**
	ēl kä'vō dä rēmōr'kyō
tow truck	**il carro attrezzi** ēl kä'rō ätre'tsē
transmission	**il cambio** ēl käm'byō
turn indicator	**la freccia** lä fre'tshä
unleaded	**senza piombo** sen'tsä pyōm'bō
valve	**la valvola** lä väl'vōlä
vehicle registration	**il libretto di circolazione**
	ēl lēbre'tō dē tshērkōlätsyō'ne
warning sign	**il triangolo** ēl trē·an'gōlō
water	**l'acqua** lä'kōō·ä
distilled -	**l'acqua distillata** lä'kōō·ä dēstēlä'tä
wheel	**la ruota** lä rōō·ō'tä
windshield wiper	**le spazzole del tergicristallo**
blades	le spä'tsōle del terjēkrēstä'lō

86

BUS, SUBWAY, TAXI

By Bus and Subway

Where's the nearest subway station?	**Dov'è la fermata della metropolitana più vicina?** dôve' lä fermä'tä de'lä metrôpōlētä'nä pyōō vētshe'nä?

INFO In Italy only Rome, Milan, and Naples have a subway system. The entrance to the subway is indicated by a sign with a white **"M"** e'me across a green background. **"M"** stands for **metropolitana**, or **metro** me'trō for short. In Venice there is of course no bus system. You can take a gondola – or a **vaporetto** väpôre'tō (motor boat), as the Venetians do.

3

Where's the *bus/ streetcar* stop for …?	**Dove ferma *l'autobus/il tram* per …?** dō've fer'mä *lou'tōbōōs/ēl träm* per …?
Which *bus/streetcar* goes to …?	**Quale *autobus/tram* va a …?** kōō-ä'le *ou'tōbōōs/träm* vä ä …?

❗	**Il numero …** ēl nōō'merō …	Number …
❗	**La linea …** lä lē'ne-ä	The … line.

When is the next *bus/streetcar* to …?	**Quando parte il prossimo *autobus/tram* per …?** kōō-än'dō par'te ēl prō'sēmo *ou'tōbōōs/träm* per …?

87

| When does the last bus/streetcar return? | **Quando riparte l'ultimo *autobus/tram*?** kōō·än'dō rēpär'te lōōl'tēmō *ou'tōbōōs/träm*? |
| Does the bus have the same schedule on *Saturdays/Sundays*? | **Di *sabato/domenica* l'autobus viaggia agli stessi orari?** dē *sä'bätō/dōme'nēkä* lou'tōbōōs vyä'jä ä'lyē ste'sē örä'rē? |

INFO Cross-country buses are often quicker and cheaper than trains. Ask about them at the local tourist bureau, since the bus companies differ from region to region. The color of the buses has nothing to do with the routes. There are bus stations in larger towns; in smaller towns, there are always special stops. One can often purchase tickets in the bus itself.

Does this *bus/ streetcar* go to …?	**Quest'*autobus/Questo* tram va a … ?** kōō·estou'tōbōōs/kōō·e'sto träm vä ä …?
Do I have to transfer to get to …?	**Per andare a … devo cambiare?** per ändä're ä … de'vō kämbyä're?
Could you tell me where I have to *get off/transfer*, please?	**Per favore, mi dice dove devo *scendere/ cambiare*?** per fävō're, mē dē'tshe dō've de'vō *shen'dere/kämbyä're*?
Where can I get a ticket?	**Dove si comprano i biglietti?** dō've sē kömprä'nō ē bēlye'tē?
I'd like a ticket to …, please.	**Un biglietto per …, per favore.** ōōn bēlye'tō per …, per fävō're.

88

INFO You can usually buy bus tickets in the **bar** bär, at the tobacconist's, and at newsstands. It's a good idea to get the **biglietti multipli** bēlye'tē mōol'tēplē (tickets valid for several trips), since they end up being cheaper than single tickets.

Are there …	**Ci sono …** tshē sō'nō …
tickets valid for several trips?	**biglietti multipli?** bēlye'tē mōol'tēplē?
day passes?	**biglietti giornalieri?** bēlye'tē jōrnälye'rē
weekly tickets?	**abbonamenti settimanali?** äbōnämen'tē setēmänä'lē?

3

Taxi!

Where can I get a taxi?	**Dov'è un posteggio di taxi?** dove' ōōn pōste'jō dē tä'ksē?
Could you order a taxi for me for … o'clock?	**Mi potrebbe chiamare un taxi per le …?** mē pōtre'be kyämä're ōōn tä'ksē per le …?
Could you take me …, please?	**…, per favore.** …, per fävō're.
to the train station	**Alla stazione** ä'lä stätsyō'ne
to the airport	**All'aeroporto** älä-erōpōr'tō
to the … Hotel	**All'hotel …** älotel' …
to the center of town	**In centro** ēn tshen'trō
to …	**A …** ä …

89

INFO To avoid nasty surprises, always make sure to take only official taxis. These will always be standing at designated taxi stands and have the appropriate taxi sign on the roof of the car.

How much is it to ...?	**Quanto costa per andare a ... ?** kōō·än'tō kō'stä per ändä're ä ...?
No, thanks, that's too expensive for me.	**No, grazie, per me è troppo caro.** nō, grä'tsē·e, per me e trō'pō kä'rō.
Is there an extra charge for baggage?	**Si paga una tariffa extra per i bagagli?** sē pä'gä ōō'nä tärē'fä ek'strä per ē bägä'lyē?
Would you *start/reset* the taxometer, please?	***Accenda/Azzeri* il tassametro, per favore!** ätshen'dä/ädze'rē ēl täsä'metrō, per fävō're.
Could you *wait/stop* here (for a moment), please?	***Aspetti/Si fermi* (un attimo) qui, per favore!** äspe'tē/sē fer'mē (ōōn ä'tēmō) kōō·ē', per fävō're.

Bus, Subway, Taxi

bus	**l'autobus** *m* lou'tōbōōs
cross-country –	**il pullman** ēl pōōl'män
– station	**la stazione dei pullman** lä stätsyō'ne dē'ē pōōlmän
city center	**il centro** ēl tshen'tro
day pass	**il biglietto giornaliero** ēl bēlye'tō jōrnälye'rō

departure	**la partenza** lä pärten'tsä
direction	**la direzione** lä dēretsyō'ne
driver	**l'autista** *m* loutē'stä
to get out	**scendere** shen'dere
last stop	**il capolinea** ēl käpōlē'ne-ä
receipt	**la ricevuta** lä rētshevōō'tä
schedule	**l'orario** lōrär'yō
to stamp *(a ticket)*	**timbrare** tēmbrä're
stop	**la fermata** lä fermä'tä
to stop	**fermare** fermä're
streetcar	**il tram** ēl träm
subway	**la metropolitana** lä metrōpōlētä'nä
taxi	**il taxi** ēl tä'ksē
– stand	**il posteggio di taxi** ēl pōste'jō dē tä'ksē
ticket	**il biglietto** ēl bēlye'tō
– (vending) machine	**il distributore automatico di biglietti** ēl dēstrēbōōtō're outōmä'tēkō dē bēlye'tē
– stamping machine	**la macchina obliteratrice** lä mä'kēnä ōblēterätrē'tshe
to transfer	**cambiare** kämbyä're
weekly ticket	**l'abbonamento settimanale** läbōnämen'tō setēmänä'le

3

HITCHHIKING

I'd like to go to …

Vorrei andare a … vōre'ē ändä're ä …

Where/Which way are you going?

Lei dove va? le'ē dō've vä?

Can you take me (part of the way) there?

Mi può dare un passaggio (per un tratto)? mē pōō-ō' dä're ōōn päsä'jō (per ōōn trä'tō)?

? ● **Dove vuole scendere?** dō've vōō-ō'le shen'dere?

Where do you want to get out?

Could you let me out here, please?

Mi faccia scendere qui, per favore. mē fä'tshä shen'dere kōō-ē', per fävo're.

Thanks for the lift.

Grazie mille per il passaggio. grä'tsē-e mē'le per ēl päsä'jo.

Food and Drink

MENÙ MENU

Antipasti *Appetizers*

acciughe *f/pl* ätshōō'ge — anchovies

affettato *m* **(misto)** — cold cut platter
äfetä'tō (mē'stō)

carciofini *m/pl* **sott'olio** — artichoke hearts in oil
kärtshōfē'nē sōtō'lyō

carpaccio *m* kärpä'tshō — thinly-sliced raw beef
tenderized with lemon juice
and oil

crostini *m/pl* **misti** — toasted bread with various
krōstē'nē mē'stē — toppings

funghi *m/pl* **sott'olio** — mushrooms in oil
fōōn'gē sōtō'lyō

gamberi *m/pl* gämbe'rē — crawfish

ostriche *f/pl* ō'strēke — oysters

prosciutto *m* prōshōō'tō — ham

  – cotto – kō'tō — cooked –

  – crudo – krōō'dō — cured –

  – con fichi freschi — – with fresh figs
  – kōn fē'kē fres'kē

  – e melone – e melō'ne — – with melon

salame *m* sälä'me — salami

sottaceti *m/pl* sōtätshe'tē — pickled vegetables

tartine *f/pl* tärtē'ne — canapés

Primi piatti   First Courses

Minestre   Soups

brodo *m* brō'dō — broth

minestra *f* mēnes'trä — soup
　– **di verdura** – dē verdōō'rä — vegetable soup

minestrone *m* mēnestrō'ne — thick vegetable soup

pastina *f* **in brodo** — broth with small pasta
pästē'nä ēn brō'dō

zuppa *f* **di pesce** — fish soup
tsōō'pä dē pe'she

Pasta e riso   Pasta and Rice

agnolotti *m/pl* änyōlō'tē — stuffed pasta

cannelloni *m/pl* känelō'nē — filled rolls of pasta

fettuccine *f/pl* fetōōtshē'ne — flat pasta

fusilli *m/pl* fōōzē'lē — spiral pasta

gnocchi *m/pl* nyō'kē — small potato dumplings

lasagne *f/pl* läzä'nye — lasagne

pasta *f* **(asciutta)** — pasta dish
pä'stä äshōō'tä

　– **al burro (in bianco)** — – with butter or olive oil
　– äl bōō'rō (ēn byän'kō)　and cheese

　– **al pomodoro** — – with tomato sauce
　äl pōmōdō'lū

　– **al ragù** – äl rägōō' — – with meat sauce

　– **alla carbonara** — – with bacon and egg
　– ä'lä kärbōnä'rä

4

95

– alla panna – ä'lä pä'nä	– with cream sauce
– al pesto – äl pe'stō	– with pesto sauce
– alle vongole	– with clams
– ä'le vōn'gōle	
penne *f/pl* pe'ne	short, straight macaroni
polenta *f* pōlen'tä	cornmeal porridge
tagliatelle *f/pl* tälyäte'le	flat pasta
vermicelli *m/pl* vermētshe'lē	thin pasta
risotto *m* rēsō'tō	rice dish
– ai funghi (porcini)	– with mushrooms
– ī fōōn'gē (pōrtshē'nē)	
– alla marinara	– with seafood
– ä'lä märēnä'rä	

Carni Meat

agnello *m* änye'lō	lamb
coniglio *m* kōnē'lyō	rabbit
maiale *m* mäyä'le	pork
maialino *m* **da latte**	suckling pig
mäyälē'nō dä lä'te	
manzo *m* män'tsō	beef
montone *m* mōntō'ne	mutton
vitello *m* vēte'lō	veal
arrosto *m* ärō'stō	roast
bistecca *f* bēste'kä	steak
braciola *f* brätshō'lä	chop
brasato *m* bräzä'tō	beef braised in wine
coscia *f* **di vitello**	leg of veal
kō'shä dē vēte'lō	

costoletta *f* kōstōle´tä	cutlet
cotoletta *f* **alla milanese**	breaded veal cutlet
kōstōle´tä ä´lä mēläne´ze	
fegato *m* fe´gätō	liver
fesa *f* **di vitello** fe´zä dē vēte´lo	veal cutlet
fettina *f* fetēnä	thinly-sliced cutlet
filetto *m* fēle´tō	filet
frattaglie *f*/*pl* frätä´lyē	organ meats
involtini *m*/*pl* ēnvōltē´nē	roulades
lombata *f* lōmbä´tä	loin
ossobuco *m* ōsōbōō´kō	knuckle of beef or veal cut
	horizontally in slices
petto *m* **di vitello**	breast of veal
pe´tō dē vēte´lō	
polpette *f*/*pl* pōlpe´te	meatballs
ragù *m* rägōō´	ragout
salsicce *f*/*pl* sälsē´tshe	sausages
scaloppine *f*/*pl* skälōpē´nē	small cutlet
spezzatino *m* spetsätē´nō	stew
spiedini *m*/*pl* **alla griglia**	shish kebab
spyedē´nē ä´lä grē´lyä	
stufato *m* stōōfä´tō	stew
vitello *m* **tonnato**	veal with tuna and
vēte´lō tōnä´tō	caper sauce

Pollame *Poultry*

anitra *f* **all'arancia**
ä'nēträ älärän'shä
duck à l'orange

fagiano *m* fäjä'nō
pheasant

faraona *f* färä-ō'nä
guinea fowl

gallina *f* gälē'nä
hen

oca *f* ō'kä
goose

petto *m* **di pollo** pe'tō dē pō'lō
chicken breast

pollo *m* pō'lō
chicken

  – arrosto – ärō'stō
    roast chicken

tacchino *m* täkē'nō
turkey

Pesce *Fish*

anguilla *f* än-gōō-ē'lä
eel

aringa *f* ärēn'gä
herring

calamari *m/pl* kälämä'rē
squid fried in rings

carpa *f* kär'pä
carp

frittura *f* **di pesce**
frētōō'rä dē pe'she
mixed fried fish

luccio *m* lōō'tshō
pike

pesce *m* **spada** pe'she spä'dä
swordfish

rombo *m* rōm'bō
turbot

salmone *m* sälmō'ne
salmon

sogliola *f* sōlyō'lä
sole

storione *m* stōryō'ne
sturgeon

tonno *m* tō'nō
tuna

triglia *f* trē'lyä
red mullet

trota trō'tä
trout

98

Crostacei e molluschi *Seafood*

aragosta *f* ärägô'stä		lobster
cozze *f/pl* kô'tse		mussels
frutti *m/pl* **di mare**		seafood
frōō'tē dē mä're		
gamberetti *m/pl* gämbere'tē		shrimps
gambero *m* gäm'berŏ		crawfish
ostriche *f/pl* ô'strēke		oysters
polpo *m* pôl'pô		octopus
vongole *f/pl* vôn'gôle		clams

Verdura e contorni *Vegetables and Side Dishes*

asparagi *m/pl* äspä'räjē		asparagus
bietole *f/pl* byetô'le		Swiss chard
carciofi *m/pl* kärtshô'fē		artichokes
– fritti – frē'tē		fried –
cavolfiore *m* kävôlfyô're		cauliflower
ceci *m/pl* tshe'tshē		chickpeas
fagioli *m/pl* fäjô'lē		beans
– bianchi di Spagna		broad –
– byän'kē dē spä'nyä		
fagiolini *m/pl* fäjôlē'nē		green –
finocchi *m/pl* fēnô'kē		fennel
funghi *m/pl* fōōn'gē		mushrooms
– coltivati – kôltēvä'tē		cultivated –
– porcini – pôrtshē'nē		porcini –
indivia *f* ēndē'vyä		endive
melanzane *f/pl* meläntsä'ne		eggplants

99

patate *f/pl* pätä′te potatoes
  – arrosto – ärō′stō – baked potato
  – fritte – frē′te French fries
  – lesse – le′se boiled potatoes
  peperonata *f* peperōnä′tä thinly sliced peppers cooked
with onions and tomatoes

peperoni *m/pl* peperō′nē peppers
piselli *m/pl* pise′lē peas
pomodori *m/pl* pōmōdō′rē tomatoes
spinaci *m/pl* spēnä′tshe spinach
zucchine *f/pl* tsōōkē′ne zucchini
  – ripiene – rēpye′ne – stuffed – au gratin

Insalate Salads

insalata *f* ēnsälä′tä salad
  – di cetrioli – dē tshetrē-ō′lē cucumber salad
  – mista – mē′stä mixed salad
  – di pomodori tomato salad
  – dē pōmōdō′rē
tonno *m* **e fagioli** salad of broad beans and tuna
tō′nō e fäjō′lē with onions

Uova Egg Dishes

frittata *f* frētä′tä omelette
tortino *m* **di carciofi** pancake with artichoke hearts
törtē′nō dē kärtshō′fē

Modi di preparazione   Methods of Preparation

affumicato äfōōmēkä'tō	smoked
a vapore ä väpo're	steamed
ai ferri ī fe're	broiled
al cartoccio äl kärtō'tshō	baked in foil
al forno äl fōr'nō	baked
alla brace ä'lä brä'tshe	grilled on a brazier
alla griglia ä'lä grē'lyä	grilled on a barbecue
allo spiedo ä'lō spye'dō	on a skewer
arrosto ärō'stō	roasted
farcito färtshē'tō	stuffed
fatto in casa fä'tō ēn kä'sä	homemade
fritto frē'tō	deep-fried
gratinato grätēnä'tō	au gratin
ripieno rēpye'nō	filled
stufato stōōfä'tō	steamed

Formaggi   Cheese

Bel paese *m* bel pä·e'ze	soft, mild cheese
formaggio *m* **grattugiato** förmä'jō grätōōjä'tō	grated cheese
gorgonzola *m* gōrgōndzō'lä	blue cheese
mozzarella *f* **di bufala** mōtsäre'lä dē bōō'fälä	buffalo mozzarella
parmigiano *m* pärmējä'nō	Parmesan cheese
pecorino *m* pekōrē'nō	sheep's cheese
stracchino *m* sträkē'nō	soft, mild cheese

4

101

Dolci Desserts

➡️ *see also Bar, Gelateria, Pasticceria (p. 104)*

budino *m* bōōdē'nō — pudding
cassata *f* käsä'tä — ice cream with candied fruits
crema *f* kre'mä — custard
crème *f* **caramel** krem kärämel' — crème caramel
macedonia *f* mätshedō'nyä — fruit salad
mousse *f* **al cioccolato** — chocolate mousse
mōōs äl tshōkōlä'tō
zabaione *m* dzäbäyō'ne — cream made of egg yolks, sugar and Marsala
zuppa *f* **inglese** — trifle
tsōō'pä ēn·gle'se

Frutta Fruit

anguria *f* ängōōr'yä — watermelon
arancia *f* ärän'tshä — orange
ciliege *f*/*pl* tshēlye'je — cherries
fico *m* 'fē'kō — fig
fragole *f*/*pl* frä'gōle — strawberries
lamponi *m*/*pl* lämpō'nē — raspberries
mela *f* me'lä — apple
melone *m* melō'ne — melon
pera *f* pe'rä — pear
pesca *f* pe'skä — peach
uva *f* ōō'vä — grape

BEVANDE BEVERAGES

Vini *Wine and Champagne*

vino *m* vē'nō	wine
– bianco – byän'kō	white –
– rosso – rō'sō	red –
– rosé – rōze'	rosé –
– da tavola – dä tä'vōlä	table –
– della casa – de'lä kä'sä	house –
– in bottiglia – ēn bōtē'lyä	– by the bottle
prosecco *m* prōse'kō	sparkling wine from the Veneto region
spumante *m* spōōmän'te	sparkling wine
dolce dōl'tsche	sweet
demi-sec demē-sek'	medium-dry
secco se'kō	dry

Altre bevande alcoliche *Other Alcoholic Drinks*

birra *f* bē'rä	beer
– alla spina – ä'lä spē'nä	draft –
– chiara – kyä'rä	blond –
– scura – skōō'rä	dark –
amaretto *m* ämäre'tō	amaretto
amaro *m* ämä'rō	bitters
grappa *f* grä'pä	strong brandy
liquore *m* lekōō-ō're	liqueur
marsala *m* märsä'lä	Marsala wine
sambuca *f* sämbōō'kä	anis liqueur
stravecchio *m* strävek'yō	well-aged cognac

4

acqua *f* **minerale**   mineral water
ä'kōō-ä mĕnerä'le
  – gassata – gäsä'tä   carbonated –
  – naturale – nätōōrä'le   non-carbonated –
aranciata *f* äräntshä'tä   orange soda
frappé *m* fräpe'   milkshake
limonata *f* lēmōnä'tä   lemon soda
spremuta *f* **di arancia**   freshly-squeezed orange juice
spremōō'tä dē ärän'tshä
spremuta *f* **di limone**   freshly-squeezed lemon juice
spremōō'tä dē lēmō'ne
succo *m* **di frutta**   fruit juice
sōō'kō dē frōō'tä
  – d'arancia – därän'tshä   orange juice
  – di mele – dē me'le   apple juice

BAR CAFÉ

caffè *m* **(espresso)**   espresso
käfe' (espre'sō)
  – corretto – kōre'tō   – with liqueur
  – lungo – lōōn'gō   – diluted with a bit of
                        water
  – macchiato – mäkyä'tō   – with milk
  – ristretto – rēstre'tō   very strong –

cappuccino *m* käpōōtshē'nō	cappuccino
camomilla *f* kämōmē'lä	camomile tea
cioccolata *f* tshōkōlä'tä	hot chocolate
latte *m* lä'te	milk
– macchiato mäkyä'tō	– with coffee
tè *m* te	hot tea
– al latte – äl lä'te	– with milk
– al limone – äl lēmō'ne	– with lemon

GELATERIA ICE CREAM

gelato *m* jelä'tō	ice cream
– affogato – äfōgä'tō	– topped with liqueur or coffee
– alla frutta – ä'lä frōō'tä	fruit –
– alla crema – ä'lä kre'mä	rich –
– con la panna – kōn lä pä'nä	– with whipped cream
– fior di latte – fyōr dē lä'te	– made with cream
ghiacciolo gyätshō'lō	popsicle
granita *f* gränē'tä	grainy kind of sherbet
semifreddo *m* semēfre'dō	semi-frozen ice cream or cake
tartufo *m* tärtōō-fō	chocolate-covered ice cream

4

105

PASTICCERIA CAKES

amaretti *m/pl* ämäre'tē	almond cookies
bignè *m* bēnye'	cream puffs
bombolone *m* bōmbōlō'ne	filled donuts
brioche *f* brē-ōsh'	croissants
ciambella *f* tshämbe'lä	fried yeast pastry
crostata *f* krōstä'tä	tart
diplomatico *m* dēplōmä'tēkō	pastry with cream and liqueur
meringa *f* merēn'gä	meringue
pan *m* **di Spagna** pän dē spä'nyä	pound cake
panna *f* **montata** pä'nä mōntä'tä	whipped cream
pasticcini *m/pl* pästētshē'nē	tea cakes
sfogliatella *f* sfōlyäte'lä	pastry filled with jam or cream
torta *f* tōr'tä	cake
– **al cioccolato** – äl tshōkōlä'tō	– chocolate
– **alla frutta** – ä'lä frōō'tä	– with fruit
– **di mandorle** – dē män'dōrle	almond –
– **di mele** – dē me'le	– with apples
– **gelato** – jelä'tō	ice cream –

INFORMATION

Is there a ... around here?	**Scusi, c'è ... qui vicino?** skōō´zē, tshe ... kōō·ē´ vētshē´nō?
a good restaurant	**un buon ristorante** ōōn bōō·ōn´ rēstōrän´te
an inexpensive restaurant	**un ristorante non troppo caro** ōōn rēstōrän´te nōn trō´pō kä´rō
a restaurant typical of the area	**un ristorante tipico** ōōn rēstōrän´te tē´pēkō
a bar	**un bar** ōōn bär
a café	**un caffè** ōōn käfe´

INFO You won't get a pizza in a **ristorante** rēstōrän´te; here, you usually order a four-course meal: **antipasto** äntēpä´stō (appetizer), **primo** prē´mō (soup or a pasta or a rice dish), **secondo** sekōn´dō (meat or fish), and **dolce** dōl´tshe (dessert). If you don't wish to eat all four courses, you can order a **secondo** or a **primo**. If you wish to have a side dish of anything with your **secondo** (which will consist of the meat or fish dish and nothing else) you must order it as well. **Coperto** kōper´tō is the cover charge for cutlery, tablecloth, and bread.

4

Could you reserve me a table for ... people for ... o'clock?	**Mi potrebbe riservare un tavolo per ... persone per le ...?** mē pōtre´be rēzervä´re ōōn tä´vōlō per ... per sō´ne per le ...?

107

INFO A **trattoria** trätōrē'ä is a more informal, inexpensive restaurant that offers dishes that are typical of the area. Recently, more expensive restaurants have begun to call themselves **trattorie** in order to suggest a rustic ambience.

A **pizzeria** pētserē'ä might only be open in the evenings since Italians don't eat **pizza** during the day. They also offer other dishes in addition to **pizza**. You can order just a **primo** prē'mō or **dolce** dōl'tshe in the **pizzeria**, something particularly popular with young people after the movies or the theater. If you feel like eating **pizza** during the day, you'll have to find a **pizzeria** that serves **pizza al taglio** pē'tsä äl tä'lyō (pizza slices), which you can eat there standing or take out.

A table for ..., please.	**Un tavolo per ... persone, per favore.**
	ōōn tä'vōlō per ... persō'ne, per fävō're.
May I have this *table/seat*?	**È libero questo *tavolo/posto*?**
	e lē'berō kōō·e'stō *tä'vōlō/pō'stō*?
Do you have a highchair?	**Avete un seggiolone?**
	äve'te ōōn sejōlō'ne?
Excuse me, where are the rest rooms?	**Scusi, dov'è la toilette?**
	skōō'zē, dōve' lä tōō·älet'?

! **Qui a *destra/sinistra*.** | Down there on the *right/left*.
● kōō·ē' ä *des'trä/sēnēs'trä*. |

WAITER!

May I see the menu, please?	**Il menù, per favore.** ēl menōō', per făvō're.

I'd like to eat something.	**Vorrei mangiare qualcosa.** vōre'ē mänjä're kōō·älkō'sä.
I'd just like something small to eat.	**Vorrei fare soltanto uno spuntino.** vōre'ē fä're sōltän'tō ōō'nō spōōnte'nō.
I just want something to drink.	**Vorrei soltanto bere qualcosa.** vōre'ē sōltän'tō be're kōō·älkō'sä.
Unfortunately we don't have much time.	**Purtroppo non abbiamo molto tempo.** pōōrtrō'pō nōn äbyä'mō mōl'tō tem'pō.

INFO During the day, you might want to try out the **tavola calda** tä'vōlä käl'dä, a kind of cafeteria where you can get inexpensive hot food at a counter. The **rosticceria** rōstētsherē'ä is also an informal type of restaurant, open only during the day. There you may get various foods such as roast chicken and vegetables or lasagne, which you can take out or sometimes eat there.

The **paninoteca** pänēnōte'kä is a relatively new kind of fast-food restaurant. You can get hot and cold **panini** pänē'nē (sandwiches) there.

4

109

? **Che cosa desidera da bere?** What would you like
kē kō'sä desē'derä dä be're? to drink?

I'd like ..., please. **Vorrei ...** vôre'ē ...

a glass of red wine **un bicchiere di vino rosso.**
ōōn bēkye're dē vē'nō rō'sō.

a bottle of beer **una bottiglia di birra.**
ōō'nä bōtē'lyä dē bē'rä.

a liter/half a liter **un/mezzo litro di vino bianco.**
of white wine ōōn/me'tsō lē'trō dē vē'nō byän'kō.

a quarter of a liter **un quarto di vino rosé.**
of rosé ōōn kōō·är'tō dē vē'nō rōze'.

a caraffe of water **una caraffa d'acqua.**
ōō'nä kärä'fä dä'kōō·ä.

a cup of coffee **una tazza di caffè.**
ōō'nä tä'tsä dē käfe'.

Do you also have **Ha anche del vino sfuso?**
wine by the glass? ä än'ke del vē'nō sfu'zō?

INFO You can order a single glass of wine only at a
bar bär. In restaurants and pizzerias you must
order wine by the 1/4, 1/2, or full liter. A **bar** is not like an
American bar; you go there for coffees and other hot and cold
beverages as well as aperitifs. If you order a **caffè** käfe', you will
get an **espresso** espre'sō; **cappuccino** käpōōtshe'nō is **espresso**
with frothed milk. In private homes you often get **caffèlatte**
käfelä'te, coffee with warm but unfrothed milk.

110

? **Che cosa desidera (mangiare)?** ke kō'sä dese'derä (mänjä're)?	What would you like to eat?	

I would like a serving of …	**Vorrei una porzione di …** vōre'ē ōō'nä pörtsyō'ne dē …
I'd like a piece of …	**Vorrei un pezzo di …** vōre'ē ōōn pe'tsō dē …
Do you have … ?	**Ha …?** ä …?
What would you recommend?	**Che cosa mi consiglia?** ke kō'sä mē kōnse'lyä?

! **Le consiglio …** le kōnse'lyō …   I can recommend …

Do you have any regional specialties?	**Quali sono le specialità della regione?** kōō·ä'lē sō'nō le spetshälētä' de'lä rejō'ne?
Do you serve …	**Avete …** äve'te …
diabetic meals?	**cibi per diabetici?** tshē'bē per dyäbe'tētshē?
special diet meals?	**cibi dietetici?** tshē'bē dyete'tētshē?
vegetarian dishes?	**piatti vegetariani?** pyä'tē vejetäryä'nē?
Can we get a children's portion?	**È possibile avere una mezza porzione per i bambini?** e pōse'bēle äve're oo'nä me'tsä pōrtsyō'ne per ē bämbē'nē?

4

111

Does it have …? I'm not allowed to eat that.	**C'è … in questo piatto? Non lo posso mangiare.** tshe … ēn kōō·e'stō pyä'tō? nōn lō pō'sō mänjä're.

❓ Che cosa prende per *antipasto/dessert*? ke kō'sä pren'de per äntēpä'stō/deser'?	Would you care for *an appetizer/some dessert*?

No, thank you, I don't care for *an appetizer/any dessert*.	***L'antipasto/Il dessert* non lo prendo, grazie.** läntēpä'stō/ēl deser' nōn lō pren'dō, grä'tsē·e.

INFO You can purchase entire cakes and tarts in the **pasticceria** pästētsherë'ä. In restaurants you can get single pieces of cakes for dessert.

Could I have … instead of …?	**Potrei avere … invece di …?** pōtre'ē äve're … ēnve'tshe dē …?

❓ Come la vuole la bistecca? kō'me lä vōō·ō'le lä bēste'kä?	How would you like your steak?

Rare.	**Al sangue.** äl sän'gōō·e.
Medium.	**Non troppo cotta, ma non al sangue.** nōn trō'pō kō'tō, mä nōn äl sän'gōō·e.
Well-done.	**Ben cotta.** ben kō'tä.
Could you bring me *another/some more* …, please?	**Per favore, mi porti ancora …** per fävō're, mē pōr'tē änkō'rä …

112

COMPLAINTS

I didn't order this. I wanted …	**Non ho ordinato questo, io volevo …** nōn ō ōrdēnä'tō kōō·e'stō, ē'ō vōle'vō …
The … is/are missing.	**Manca/Mancano ancora …** män'kä/mänkä'nō ankō'rä …

INFO At the **bar** or **bar pasticceria** bär pästētsherē'ä you can get a typically Italian breakfast: **cappuccino e brioche** käpōōtshē'nō e brē·ōsh' or **pasta** pä'stä (a piece of cake or pastry). You can also get something small there for lunch. You must almost always pay for your meal at the cashier's first; you must present your **scontrino** skōntrē'nō (receipt) to get your meal or drink. Usually one eats and drinks while standing at the counter. But in the summer, a **bar** might put some tables outside. The prices will differ according to whether you are eating at the counter or at a table with service. A **bar gelateria** bär jelätere'ä will produce its own ice cream; a **bar pasticceria** bär pästētsherē'ä offers its own home-made cakes.

4

The meat hasn't been cooked enough.	**La carne non è abbastanza cotta.** lä kär'ne nōn e äbästän'tsä kō'tä.
Could you take it back, please?	**Lo riporti indietro, per favore.** lo repor'te ēndye'trō, per fävō're?

113

THE CHECK, PLEASE

Could I have the check, please?	**Il conto, per favore.** ēl kōn'tō, per fävo're.
I'd like a receipt.	**Vorrei la ricevuta.** vōre'ē lä rētshevōo'tä.
We'd like separate checks, please.	**Conti separati, per favore.** kōn'tē sepärä'tē, per fävo're.

INFO When Italians go out to eat with friends, they usually get one bill and figure out each one's share. Going Dutch is called **pagare alla romana** pägä're ä'lä rōmä'nä.

May I treat you?	*La/Ti* **posso invitare?** lä/tē po'sō ēnvētä're?
You're my guest today.	**Oggi** *è/sei* **mio ospite.** o'jē *e/se'ē* mē'o o'spite.

? **È stato di** *Suo/vostro* **gradimento?**
e stä'tō dē *sōo'o/vos'trō* grädēmen'tō?   Did you enjoy your meal?

It was very nice, thank you.	**Grazie, era davvero molto buono.** grä'tsē·e, e'rä däve'rō mōl'tō bōo·o'nō.
I think there must be some mistake here.	**Mi sembra che ci sia un errore.** mē sem'brä ke tshē sē'ä ōon erō're.

INFO The **birreria** bērērē'ä is only open in the evening. There you can get cold and sometimes simple warm dishes. These informal restaurants offer a large selection of beers. In general, beer in Italy is rather expensive, and imported beers are more expensive than Italian ones.

We didn't order this.	**Questo non lo abbiamo ordinato.** kōō·e'sto nōn lō äbyä'mō ōrdēnä'tō.
Thank you very much.	**Molte grazie.** mōl'te grä'tsē·e.

DINING WITH FRIENDS

Enjoy your meal!	**Buon appetito!** bōō·on' äpetē'tō!
Cheers!	**(Alla) salute!** (ä'lä) sälōō'te!

? *Le/Ti piace?* le/tē pyä'tshe?   How do you like it?

It's very good, thank you.	**È molto buono, grazie.** e mōl'tō bōō·ō'nō, grä'tsē·e.
That's exquisite.	**Questo è veramente squisito.** kōō·e'sto e verämen'te skōōēzē'tō.
What's that?	**Che cos'è?** ke kōse'?
Would you pass me the ..., please?	**Mi** *potrebbe/potresti* **passare ...?** mē *pōtre'be/pōtre'stē* päsä're ...?

4

115

? Ancora un po' di …?
   änkō'rä ōōn pō dē …?

Would you like some
more?

Yes, please.	**Sì, volentieri.** sē, völentye'rē.
No, thanks, not right now.	**Per il momento no, grazie.** per ēl mōmen'tō nō, grä'tsē-e.
No, thank you, I'm full.	**Grazie, ma sono già ♂ sazio/♀ sazia.** grä'tsē-e, mä sō'nō jä ♂ sä'tsyō/♀ sä'tsyä.
Do you mind if I smoke?	**La/Ti disturbo se fumo?** lä/tē dēstoor'bō sē fōō'mō?
Thank you for inviting me.	**Grazie per l'invito.** grä'tsē-e per lēnvē'tō.
It was delicious.	**È stato eccellente.** e stä'tō etshelen'te.

➡ *see also: Please, Thank you (p. 25)*

Food and drink

appetizer	**l'antipasto** läntēpä'sto
artificial sweetener	**il dolcificante** ēl döltshēfēkän'te
ashtray	**il posacenere** ēl pōzätshe'nere
available	**libero** lē'berō
bar	**il bar** ēl bär
beer	**la birra** lä bē'rä
bottle	**la bottiglia** lä bōtē'lyä
– opener	**l'apribottiglie** *m* läprēbōtē'lye
bread	**il pane** ēl pä'ne

– roll	**il panino** ēl pänē'nō
whole-wheat –	**il pane integrale** ēl pä'ne ēntegrä'le
breakfast	**la colazione** lä kōlätsyō'ne
to bring	**portare** pōrtä're
butter	**il burro** ēl bōō'rō
café	**il bar, la pasticceria, il caffè**
	ēl bär, lä pästētsherē'ä, ēl käfe'
cake	**la torta** lä tōr'tä
carafe	**la caraffa** lä kärä'fä
cheese	**il formaggio** ēl fōrmä'jō
children's portion	**la mezza porzione** lä me'tsä pōrtsyō'ne
(hot) chocolate	**la cioccolata** lä tshōkōlä'tä
cocoa	**il cacao** ēl käkä'ō
coffee	**il caffè** ēl käfe'
black –	**il caffè nero** ēl käfe' ne'rō
decaffeinated –	**il caffè decaffeinato**
	ēl käfe' dekäfe-ēnä'tō
regular –	**il caffè alla tedesca**
	ēl käfe' ä'lä tedes'kä
– with milk	**il caffelatte, il caffè macchiato**
	ēl käfelä'te, ēl käfe' mäkyä'tō
– with sugar	**il caffè zuccherato**
	ēl käfe' tsōōkerä'tō
cold	**freddo** fre'dō
– cut platter	**l'affettato** läfetä'tō
cookies	**i biscotti** ē bēskō'tē
corkscrew	**il cavatappi** ēl kävätä'pē
course	**il piatto** ēl pyä'tō
first –	**il primo** ēl prē'mō

4

117

second –	**il secondo** ĕl sekōn'dō
cream	**la panna** lä pä'nä
crudités	**le verdure crude** le verdōō're krōō'de
cup	**la tazza** lä tä'tsä
cutlery	**le posate** le pōsä're
dessert	**il dolce** ĕl dōl'tshe
diabetic	**il diabetico** ĕl dyäbe'tēkō
diet	**la dieta** lä dē·e'tä
dinner	**la cena** lä tshe'nä
dish	**il piatto** ĕl pyä'tō
dough	**la pasta** lä pä'stä
drink	**la bevanda** lä bevän'dä
to drink	**bere** be're
drinks menu	**la carta delle bevande**
	lä kär'tä de'le bevän'de
to eat	**mangiare** mänjä're
egg	**l'uovo,** *pl:* **le uova**
	lōō·ō'vō, *pl:* le ōō·ō'vä
fried –	**l'uovo al tegame**
	lōō·ō'vō äl tegä'me
hard-boiled –	**l'uovo sodo** lōō·ō'vō sō'dō
scrambled –	**le uova strapazzate**
	leōō·ō'vä sträpätsä'te
soft-boiled –	**l'uovo alla coque** lōō·ō'vō ä'lä kōk
excellent	**eccellente** etshelen'te
fat	**grasso** grä'sō
filling	**il ripieno** ĕl rēpye'nō
fish	**il pesce** ĕl pe'she
food	**il mangiare** ĕl mänjä're

fork	**la forchetta** lä forke'tä
fresh	**fresco** fres'kō
fruit	**la frutta** lä frōō'tä
to be full	**essere sazio** e'sere sä'tsyō
garlic	**l'aglio** (ä'lyō)
glass	**il bicchiere** ēl bēkye're
grease	**il grasso** ēl grä'sō
guest	**l'ospite** *m, f* lō'spēte
ham	**il prosciutto** ēl prōshōō'tō
hard	**duro** dōō'rō
homemade	**fatto in casa** fä'tō ēn kä'sä
honey	**il miele** ēl mye'le
hot *(temperature)*	**caldo** käl'dō
hot *(spicy)*	**piccante** pēkän'te
to be hungry	**avere fame** äve're fä'me
ice (cube)	**il (cubetto di) ghiaccio** ēl (kōōbe'tō dē) gyä'tshō
to invite	**invitare** ēnvētä're
jam	**la marmellata** lä märmelä'tä
ketchup	**il ketchup** ēl ket'shäp
knife	**il coltello** ēl kōlte'lō
lean	**magro** mäg'rō
light food	**gli alimenti dietetici** lyē älēmen'tē dyete'tētshē
lunch	**il pranzo** ēl prän'tsō
margarine	**la margarina** lä märgäre'na
mayonnaise	**la maionese** lä mäyōnē'ze
meat	**la carne** lä kär'ne
menu	**il menù** ēl menōō'

4

milk	**il latte**	ēl lä'te
mineral water	**l'acqua minerale**	lä'kōō·ä mēnerä'le
non-carbonated –	**l'acqua minerale naturale**	
	lä'kōō·ä mēnerä'le nätōōrä'le	
carbonated –	**l'acqua minerale gassata**	
	lä'kōō·ä mēnerä'le gäsä'tä	
mushrooms	**i funghi**	ē fōōn'gē
napkin	**il tovagliolo**	ēl tōvälyō'lō
non-alcoholic	**analcolico**	änälkō'lēkō
oil	**l'olio**	lō'lyō
olive –	**l'olio d'oliva**	lō'lyō dōlē'vä
onion	**la cipolla**	lä tshēpō'lä
to order	**ordinare**	ōrdēnä're
to pay	**pagare**	pägä're
pepper	**il pepe**	ēl pe'pe
peppermint tea	**l'infuso di menta**	lēnfōō'zō dē men'tä
piece	**il pezzo**	ēl pe'tsō
pizza	**la pizza**	lä pē'tsä
place setting	**il coperto**	ēl kōper'tō
place, seat	**il posto**	ēl pō'stō
portion	**la porzione**	lä pōrtsyō'ne
to recommend	**consigliare**	kōnsēlyä're
to reserve	**prenotare**	prenōtä're
restaurant	**il ristorante**	ēl rēstōrän'te
restroom	**la toilette**	lä tōō·älet'
salad	**l'insalata**	lēnsälä'tä
salt	**il sale**	ēl sä'le
sandwich	**il panino (imbottito)**	
	ēl pänē'nō (ēmbōtē'tō)	

sauce *(in general)*	**la salsa** lä säl'sä	
sauce *(for pasta)*	**il sugo** ēl sōō'gō	
seasoned	**condito** kōndē'tō	
to get separate checks	**pagare separatamente** pägä're sepärätämen'te	
slice	**la fetta** lä fe'tä	
soft	**morbido** mōr'bēdō	
soup *(in general)*	**la zuppa** lä tsōō'pä	
soup *(with pasta or rice)*	**la minestra** lä mēnes'trä	
sour *(culinary in general)*	**agro** ä'grō	
sour *(of milk products)*	**acido** ä'tshēdō	
special of the day	**il piatto del giorno** ēl pyä'tō del jōr'nō	
speciality	**la specialità** lä spetshälētä'	
spice	**le spezie** le spe'tsye	
spoon	**il cucchiaio** ēl kōōkyä'yō	
straw *(for drinking)*	**la cannuccia** lä känōō'tshä	
sugar	**lo zucchero** lō tsōō'kerō	
sweet	**dolce** dōl'tshe	
table	**il tavolo** ēl tä'vōlō	
to taste good	**piacere** pyätshe're	
tea	**il tè** ēl te	
camomile –	**la camomilla** lä kämōmē'lä	
fruit –	**la tisana di frutta** lä tēzä'nä dē frōō'tä	
–spoon	**il cucchiaino** ēl kōōkyä·ē'nō	
tender	**tenero** ten'erō	

4

121

to be thirsty	**avere sete** äve're se'te
tip	**la mancia** lä män'tshä
toast	**il toast** ēl tōst
vegetables	**la verdura** lä verdōō'rä
vegetarian	**vegetariano** vejetäryä'nō
vinegar	**l'aceto** lätshe'tō
waiter	**il cameriere** ēl kämerye're
waitress	**la cameriera** lä kämerye'rä
water	**l'acqua** lä'kōō-ä
wine	**il vino** ēl vē'nō
zwieback	**la fetta biscottata** lä fe'tä bēskōtä'tä

Sightseeing

TOURIST INFORMATION

May I have …
Vorrei … vȯre'ē …

a list of hotels?
un annuario degli alberghi.
ōōn änōō·är'yō del'yē älber'gē.

a map of the area?
una cartina della zona.
ōō'nä kärtē'nä de'lä dzō'nä.

a brochure
about … ?
un depliant su …
ōōn deplē·än' sōō …

a street map?
una pianta della città.
ōō'nä pyän'tä de'lä tshētä'.

a subway map?
una cartina della metropolitana.
ōō'nä kärtē'nä de'lä metrōpōlētä'nä.

a schedule of
events?
un programma delle manifestazioni.
ōōn prōgrä'mä de'le
mänēfestätsyō'nē

Could you reserve
a room for me?
Mi potrebbe prenotare una camera?
mē pōtre'be prenōtä're ōō'nä kä'merä?

Are there *sightseeing
tours/guided walking
tours of the city?*
**Ci sono *giri turistici organizzati della
città/delle visite guidate?*** tshē sō'nō
jē're tōōrē'stētshē ōrgänēdzä'tē de'lä tshētä'/de'le vē'zēte gōō·ēdä'te?

How much does the
sightseeing tour cost?
**Quanto costa il biglietto per il giro
turistico della città?** kōō·än'tō kō'stä ēl
bēlye'tō per ēl jē'rō tōōrē'stēkō de'lä
tshētä'?

How long does the sightseeing tour last?	**Quanto dura il giro turistico della città?** kōō·än'tō dōō'rä ēl jē'rō tōōrē'stēkō de'lä tshētä'?
I'd like *a ticket/two tickets* for the walking tour of the city, please.	**Un biglietto/Due biglietti per la visita guidata, per favore.** ōōn bēlye'tō/dōō'e bēlye'tē per lä vē'zētä gōō·ēdä'tä, per fävō're.
I'd like to visit …	**Vorrei visitare …** vōre'ē vēzētä're …
Please reserve *a place/two places* on tomorrow's excursion for *me/us.*	**Un biglietto/Due biglietti per la gita di domani per *me/noi*, per favore.** ōōn bēlye'tō/dōō'e bēlye'tē, per lä jē'tä dē dōmä'nē per *me/nō·ē*, per fävō're.
Where/When do we meet?	**Dove/Quando ci troviamo?** kōō·än'dō/dō've tshē trōvyä'mō?
Will we also be visiting … ?	**Andiamo a vedere anche …?** ändyä'mō ä vede're än'ke …?
Will we also have some free time?	**Abbiamo tempo libero a disposizione?** äbyä'mō tem'pō lē'berō ä dēspōzētsyō'ne?
When do we start?	**A che ora si parte?** ä ke ō'rä sē pär'te?
When do we get back?	**A che ora ritorniamo?** a ke ō'rä rētōrnyä'mō?

5

➡ *Hotel reservation: Accommodations (S. 34), Asking the way: On the Way (S. 54), Public transportation: Bus, Subway, Taxi (S. 87)*

SIGHTSEEING, EXCURSIONS

When is … *open/closed*?	**A che ora apre/chiude …?** ä ke ōˈrä äˈpre/kyōōˈde …?
What's the admission charge?	**Quanto costa il biglietto d'ingresso?** kōō·änˈtō kōˈstä ēl bēlyeˈtō dēngreˈsō?
How much does the guided tour cost?	**Quanto costa la visita guidata?** kōō·änˈtō kōˈstä lä vēˈzētä gōō·ēdäˈtä?
Is there a discount for …	**C'è una riduzione per …** tshe ōōˈnä rēdōōtsyōˈne per …

families?	**famiglie?** fämēˈlye?
groups?	**gruppi?** grōōˈpē?
children?	**bambini?** bämbēˈnē?
senior citizens?	**anziani?** ändzyäˈnē?
students?	**studenti?** stōōdenˈtē?

INFO When visiting churches and monasteries, you should wear appropriate clothing (something that covers your shoulders and knees). It is possible that someone wearing shorts or something with an open neckline might not be allowed into the building.

Do you also have tours in English?	**C'è una guida che parla inglese?** tshe ōōˈnä gōō·ēˈdä ke pärˈlä ēnˈgleˈse?
When does the tour begin?	**Quando inizia la visita guidata?** kōō·änˈdō ēnēˈtsyä lä vēˈzēta gōō·ēdäˈtä?

126

| One ticket/ Two tickets, please. | **Un biglietto/Due biglietti**, per favore. |
| | ōōn bēlye'tō/dōō'e bēlye'tē, per fävo're. |

Two adults and two children, please.

Due adulti e due bambini, per favore.
dōō'e ädōōl'tē e dōō'e bämbē'nē, per fävo're.

Are you allowed to *take pictures/make a video*?

Si possono fare *fotografie/delle riprese filmate*? sē pō'sōnō fä're fōtōgräfē'e de'le rēpre'se fēlmä'te?

What *building/ monument* is that?

Che *edificio/monumento* è questo? ke edēfē'tshō/mōnōōmen'tō e kōō·e'stō?

When was ... built?

Quando è stato costruito ...? kōō·än'dō e stä'tō kōstrōō·ē'tō ...?

Do you have a *catalog/guide*?

C'è *un catalogo/una guida*? tshe ōōn kätä'lōgō/ōō'nä gōō·ē'dä?

Do you have a ... of that picture?

Avete ... del quadro? äve'tē ... del kōō·ä'drō?

slide	**una diapositiva** ōō'nä dē·äpōzētē'vä
poster	**un poster** ōōn pō'ster
postcard	**una cartolina** ōō'nä kärtōlē'nä

Sightseeing, Excursions

abbey	**l'abbazia** läbätsē'ä
alley	**il vicolo** ēl vē'kōlō
altar	**l'altare** *m* lältä're

5

127

amphitheater	**l'anfiteatro** länfētē·ä'trō
antique	**antico** äntē'kō
antiquity	**l'antichità** läntēkētä'
aqueduct	**l'acquedotto** läkōō·edō'tō
arcarde	**l'arcata** lärkä'tä
arch	**l'arco** lär'kō
archeological find	**i reperti archeologici**
	ē reper'tē ärke·ōlō'jētshē
archeology	**l'archeologia** lärke·ōlōjē'ä
architect	**l'architetto** lärkēte'tō
architecture	**l'architettura** lärkētetōō'rä
area	**la zona** lä dzō'nä
arena	**l'arena** läre'nä
art	**l'arte** *f* lär'te
– collection	**la collezione di quadri**
	lä kōletsyō'ne dē kōō·ä'drē
artist	**l'artista** *m, f* lärtē'stä
atrium	**l'atrio** lä'trē·ō
avenue	**il viale** ēl vyä'le
baptismal font	**il fonte battesimale**
	ēl fōn'te bätezēmä'le
baroque	**il barocco** ēl bärō'kō
basilica	**la basilica** lä bäzē'lēkä
bell	**la campana** lä kämpä'nä
– tower	**il campanile** ēl kämpänē'le
bridge	**il ponte** ēl pōn'te
brochure	**il depliant** ēl deplē·än'
building	**la costruzione** lä kōstrōōtsyō'ne
bust	**il busto** ēl bōō'stō

Byzantine	**bizantino** bēdzäntē'nō
capital	**la capitale** lä käpētä'le
castle	**il castello** ēl käste'lō
catacombs	**le catacombe** le kätäkōm'be
cathedral	**la cattedrale, il duomo** lä kätedrä'le, ēl dōō·ō'mō
Catholic	**cattolico** kätō'lēkō
cave	**la grotta** lä grō'tä
ceiling	**il soffitto** ēl sōfē'tō
cemetery	**il cimitero** ēl tshēmēte'rō
century	**il secolo** ēl se'kōlō
chapel	**la cappella** lä käpe'lä
chimes	**il carillon** ēl kärēyōn'
choir	**il coro** ēl kō'rō
Christian	**cristiano** krēstyä'nō
church	**la chiesa** lä kye'zä
– service	**la messa** la me'sä
city	**la città** lä tshētä'
– center	**il centro** ēl tshen'trō
– district	**il quartiere** ēl kōō·ärtye're
– gate	**la porta della città** lä pōrtä de'lä tshētä'
– hall	**il municipio** ēl mōōnētshē'pyō
historical part of the –	**il centro storico, la città vecchia** ēl tshen'trō stō'rēkō, lä tshētä' ve'kyä
map of the –	**la cartina della città** lä kärtē'nä de'lä tshētä
– square	**la piazza** lä pyä'tsä

5

129

– walls	**le mura (della città)**
	le mōō'rä (de'lä tshētä)
Classicism	**il classicismo** ēl kläsētshēz'mō
cloister	**il chiostro** ēl kyōs'trō
closed	**chiuso** kyōō'sō
coat-of-arms	**lo stemma** lō ste'mä
column	**la colonna** lä kōlō'nä
contemporary	**contemporaneo** kōntempōrä'ne-ō
convent	**il convento** ēl kōnven'tō
copy	**la copia** lä kō'pyä
Corinthian	**corinzio** kōrēn'tsyō
court	**la corte** lä kōr'te
courtyard	**il cortile** ēl kōrtē'le
cross	**la croce** lä krō'tshe
crucifix	**il crocefisso** ēl krōtshefē'sō
crypt	**la cripta** lä krēp'tä
cupola	**la cupola** lä kōō'pōlä
Doric	**dorico** dō'rēkō
drawing	**il disegno** ēl dēzen'yō
emperor	**l'imperatore** lēmperätō're
empress	**l'imperatrice** lēmperätrē'tshe
era	**l'epoca** le'pōkä
Etruscan	**etrusco** etrōō'skō
excavations	**gli scavi** lyē skä've
excursion	**la gita** lä jē'tä
exhibition	**la mostra** lä mōs'trä
façade	**la facciata** lä fätshä'tä
forest	**il bosco** ēl bō'skō
fortress	**la fortezza** lä fōrte'tsä

130

fountain	**la fontana**	lä fōntä'nä
fresco	**l'affresco**	läfre'sko
gable	**il frontone, il timpano**	ēl frōntō'ne, ēl tēm'pänō
garden	**il giardino**	ēl järdē'nō
gate	**la porta**	lä pōr'tä
glass	**il vetro**	ēl ve'trō
gorge	**la gola**	lä gō'lä
Gothic	**gotico**	gō'tēkō
Greek	**greco**	gre'kō
Greeks	**i greci**	ē gre'tshē
hall *(large room)*	**la sala**	lä sä'lä
harbor	**il porto**	ēl pōr'tō
hill	**la collina**	lä kōlē'nä
history	**la storia**	lä stōr'yä
inscription	**la scritta**	lä skrē'tä
Ionic	**ionico**	ē-ō'nēkō
island	**l'isola**	lē'zōlä
king	**il re**	ēl re
lake	**il lago**	ēl lä'gō
landscape	**il paesaggio**	ēl pä-ezä'jō
marble	**il marmo**	ēl mär'mō
market	**il mercato**	ēl merkä'tō
covered –	**il mercato coperto**	ēl merkä'tō kōper'tō
Middle Ages	**il medioevo**	ēl medyō-e'vō
model *(figurine)*	**il modello**	ēl mōde'lō
modern	**moderno**	mōder'nō
monastery	**il monastero**	ēl mōnäste'rō

5

131

monument	**il monumento** ēl mōnōōmen'tō	
mosaic	**il mosaico** ēl mōzä'ēkō	
mountain	**la montagna** lä mōntän'yä	
mural	**la pittura murale** lä pētōō'rä mōōrä'le	
museum	**il museo** ēl mōōze'ō	
folklore –	**il museo delle tradizioni popolari** ēl mōōze'ō de'le trädētsyō'nē pōpōlä'rē	
national park	**il parco nazionale** ēl pär'kō nätsēōnä'le	
nature preserve	**la zona protetta** lä dzō'nä prōte'tä	
open	**aperto** äper'tō	
opera	**l'opera** lō'perä	
organ	**l'organo** lôrgä'nō	
original	**l'originale** m lōrējēnä'le	
painter	**il pittore** ēl pētō're	
painting	**il quadro** ēl kōō·ä'drō	
palace	**il palazzo** ēl pälä'tsō	
park	**il parco** ēl pär'kō	
pedestrian zone	**la zona pedonale, la zona blu** lä dzō'nä pedōnä'le, lä dzō'nä blōō	
peninsula	**la penisola** lä penē'zōlä	
to take photographs	**fotografare** fōtōgräfä're	
picture	**il quadro** ēl kōō·ä'drō	
pilgrim	**il pellegrino** ēl pellegrē'nō	
pillar	**il pilastro** ēl pēläs'trō	
(floor) plan	**la pianta** lä pyän'tä	
planetarium	**il planetario** ēl plänetär'yō	
poet	**il poeta** ēl po·e'tä	
porcelain	**la porcellana** lä pōrtshelä'nä	

portal	**il portale** ĕl pōrtä′le
portrait	**il ritratto** ĕl rēträ′tō
pottery	**l'arte della ceramica**
	lär′te de′lä tsherä′mēkä
queen	**la regina** lä rejē′nä
to reconstruct	**ricostruire** rēkōströō-ē′re
relief	**il rilievo** ĕl rēlē̄e′vō
religion	**la religione** lä relējō′ne
remains	**i resti** ē re′stē
Renaissance	**il Rinascimento** ĕl rēnäshēmen′tō
to restore	**restaurare** restourä′re
river	**il fiume** ĕl fyōō′me
Roman	**romano** rōmä′nō
Romanesque	**romanico** rōmä′nēkō
Romans	**i romani** ē rōmä′nē
romantic	**romantico** rōmän′tēkō
ruin	**la rovina** lä rōvē′nä
sanctuary *(place of pilgrimage)*	**il santuario** ĕl säntōō-är′yō
sandstone	**la pietra arenaria** lä pye′trä ärenär′yä
sarcophagus	**il sarcofago** ĕl särkō′fägō
sculptor	**lo scultore** lō skōōltō′re
sculpture	**la scultura** lä skōōltōō′rä
statue	**la statua** lä stä′tōō-ä
style	**lo stile** lō stē′le
surrounding area	**i dintorni** e dentor′ne
synagogue	**la sinagoga** lä sēnägō′gä
temple	**il tempio** ĕl tem′pyō
theater	**il teatro** ĕl te-ä′trō

5

133

tomb	**la tomba** lä tömb'bä
tour of the city/town	**la visita guidata della città** lä vē'zētä gōō-ēdä'tä de'lä tshētä'
tourist information office	**l'ufficio informazioni turistiche** lōōfē'tshō ēnförmätsyō'nē tōōrē'stēke
tower	**la torre** lä tô're
treasure chamber	**il tesoro** ēl tesō'rō
triumphal arch	**l'arco di trionfo** lär'kō dē trē-ōn'fō
university	**l'università** lōōnēversētä'
valley	**la valle** lä vä'le
vase	**il vaso** ēl vä'zō
vault	**la volta** lä vōl'tä
to videotape	**filmare** fēlmä're
view	**il panorama** ēl pänörä'mä
vineyard	**il vigneto** ēl vēnye'tō
to visit	**visitare** vēzētä're
volcano	**il vulcano** ēl vōōlkä'nō
wall	**il muro** ēl mōō·rō
waterfall	**la cascata** lä käskä'tä
window	**la finestra** lä fēne'strä
wine-tasting	**la degustazione del vino** lä degōōstätsyō'ne del vē'nō
wing	**l'ala** lä'lä
woodcarving (*as a handicraft*)	**l'intaglio** lēntä'lyō
woodcarving (*figure*)	**la scultura in legno** lä skōōltōō'rä ēn le'nyō
work	**l'opera** lō'perä
zoo	**lo zoo** lō dzō'ō

134

INFO In Italy there are a great many wildlife preserves that protect rare animal and plant species. There are bears and wolves in the **Parco Nazionale degli Abruzzi** pär'kō nätsyōnä'le de'lye äbrōō'tse. The **Parco del Pollino** pär'kō del pōle'nō is wellknown for its rare plant forms.

Plants

almond tree	**il mandorlo**	ēl män'dôrlō
beech tree	**il faggio**	ēl fä'jō
broom	**la ginestra**	lä jēnes'trä
chestnut tree	**il castagno**	ēl kästä'nyō
cork oak tree	**il sughero**	ēl sōō'gerō
cypress tree	**il cipresso**	ēl tshēpre'sō
grape vines	**le viti**	le vē'tē
larch tree	**il larice**	ēl lä'rētshe
lemon tree	**il limone**	ēl lēmō'ne
maritime pine tree	**il pino marittimo**	ēl pē'nō märē'tēmō
oak tree	**la quercia**	lä kōō·er'tshä
oleander	**l'oleandro**	lōle·än'drō
olive tree	**l'ulivo**	lōōlē'vō
orange tree	**l'arancio**	lärän'tshō
spruce tree	**il pino**	ēl pē'nō
stone/umbrella pine tree	**il pino a ombrello**	ēl pē'nō ä ōmbre'lō
walnut tree	**il noce**	ēl nō'tshe

5

135

Animals

boar	**il cinghiale** ēl tshēn·gyä′le
butterfly	**la farfalla** lä färfä′lä
cat	**il gatto** ēl gä′tō
cow	**la mucca** lä mōō′kä
dog	**il cane** ēl kä′ne
donkey	**l'asino** lä′sēnō
eagle	**l'aquila** lä′kōō·ēlä
fox	**la volpe** lä vōl′pe
horse	**il cavallo** ēl kävä′lō
ibex *(mountain goat)*	**lo stambecco** lō stämbe′kō
mule	**il mulo** ēl mōō′lō
snake	**la serpe, il serpente** lä ser′pe, ēl serpen′te
wolf	**il lupo** ēl lōōpō

136

Shopping

BASIC PHRASES

Where can I get …? **Dove posso trovare …?**
dōve pŏ'sō trōvä're …

! **Dica, prego!** dē'kä, pre'gō! May I help you?

? **Posso aiutarLa?** pŏ'sō äyōōtär'lä? May I help you?

I'm just looking, **Grazie, ma vorrei soltanto dare**
thanks. **un'occhiata.** grä'tsē-ē, mä vōre'ē
sōltän'tō dä're ōōnōkyä'tä.

I'm being helped, **Mi stanno già servendo.**
thanks. mē stä'nō jä serven'dō.

I'd like … **Vorrei …** vōre'ē …

Please give me … **Per favore, mi dia …**
per fävō're, mē dē'ä …

a can of … **un barattolo** (in general)/**una lattina**
(drink) **di …** ōōn bärä'tōlō/ōō'nä läte'nä
dē …

a bottle of … **una bottiglia di …**
ōō'nä bōtē'lyä dē …

a jar of … **un barattolo di …** ōōn bärä'tōlō dē …

a package of … **un pacco di …** ōōn pä'kō dē …

a box of … **una scatola di …** ōō'nä skä'tōlä dē …

a tube of … **un tubetto di …** ōōn tōōbe'tō dē …

! **Mi dispiace, ma … è finito.** I'm sorry, but we're
mē dēspyä'tshe, mä … e fēnē'tō. out of …

| How much is/are ...? | **Quanto costa/costano ...?** |
| | kōō·än'tō *kō'stä/kō'stäno* ...? |

| Could you show me ..., please? | **Per favore, mi fa vedere ...?** |
| | per fävō're, mē fä vede're ...? |

| That's not quite what I'm looking for. | **Questo non mi piace tanto.** |
| | kōō·e'stō nōn mē pyä'tshe tän'tō. |

| Could you show me something else? | **Mi può mostrare qualcos'altro?** |
| | mē pōō·ō' mōsträ're kōō·älkōsäl'trō? |

| I'd like something a little less expensive. | **Vorrei qualcosa di meno caro.** |
| | vōre'ē kōō·älkō'sä dē me'nō kä'rō. |

| I'll have to think about it. | **Ci devo pensare ancora un po'.** |
| | tshē de'vō pensä're änkō'rä ōōn pō. |

| I like this. I'll take it. | **Mi piace, lo prendo.** |
| | mē pyä'tshe, lō pren'dō. |

? **Desidera altro?** dese'derä äl'trō? Will there be anything else?

| That's all, thank you. | **Grazie, è tutto.** grä'tsē·e, e tōō'tō. |

| Can I pay with this credit card? | **Posso pagare con questa carta di credito?** pō'so pagä're kōn kōō·e'sta kär'tä dē kre'dētō? |

| May I have a (plastic) bag for it? | **Ha un sacchetto (di plastica), per favore?** ä ōōn säke'tō (dē plä'stēkä), per fävō're? |

139

INFO When you buy something, you should make sure you get the **scontrino fiscale** skōntrë'nō fëskä'le (receipt) and hold on to it at least until you are 100 meters away from the store. In order to avoid tax evasion, the **Guardia di Finanza** gōō·är'dyä dē fēnän'tsä (finance police) has the right to check and make sure that the bill has been added up accurately. The **scontrino** is the proof that the owner of the store has registered his earnings properly. If you are not in possession of the **scontrino**, you could be fined as well.

Could you wrap it up well for my return trip, please?	**Me lo può incartare bene per il viaggio?** me lō pōō·ò' ēnkärtä're be'ne per ēl vyä'jō?
How much does it cost?	**Quanto costa?** kōō·än'tō kō'stä?
This is broken. Could you repair it?	**È rotto, lo può riparare?** e rō'tō, lō pōō·ò' rēpärä're?
When will it be ready?	**Per quando sarà pronto?** per kōō·än'dō särä' prōn'tō?
I'd like to *exchange/return* this.	**Lo vorrei *cambiare/dare indietro*.** lō vōre'ē *kämbyä're/dä're ēndye'trō*.
I'd like a refund, please.	**Vorrei riavere indietro i soldi.** vōre'ē rē·äve're ēndye'trō ē sōl'dē.
Sorry, but you haven't given me enough change. I'm short …	**Mi ha dato …. di meno.** mē ä dä'tō … dē me'nō.

(plastic) bag	**il sacchetto (di plastica)** ēl säke'tō (dē plä'stēkä)
better	**migliore** mēlyō're
big	**grande** grän'de
bigger	**più grande** pyōō grän'de
to buy	**comprare** kômprä're
can	**la lattina** lä lätē'nä
cheaper	**meno caro** me'nō kä'rō
to cost	**costare** kôstä're
credit card	**la carta di credito** lä kär'tä dē kre'dētō
to exchange	**cambiare** kämbyä're
expensive	**caro** kä'rō
gift	**il regalo** ēl regä'lō
to give	**dare** dä're
money	**i soldi** ē sôl'dē
pack	**il pacchetto** ēl päke'tō
package	**il pacco** ēl pä'kō
receipt	**la ricevuta** lä rētshevōō'tä
to return	**dare indietro** dä're ēndye'trō
self-service	**il self-service** ēl self-ser'vēs
to show	**mostrare** mōsträ're
small	**piccolo** pē'kōlō
smaller	**più piccolo** pyōō pē'kōlō
special offer	**l'offerta speciale** lôfer'tä spetshä'le
to take	**prendere** pren'dere
too	**troppo** trô'pō
(shop) window	**la vetrina** lä vetrē'nä

Colors and Patterns

beige	**beige** *(inv)* bej
black	**nero** ne′rō
blue	**blu** *(inv)* blōō
brown	**marrone** märō′ne
checked	**a quadri** ä kōō-ä′drē
colorful	**colorato** kōlōrä′tō
dark	**scuro** skōō′rō
gold	**dorato** dōrä′tō
gray	**grigio** grē′jō
green	**verde** ver′de
light	**chiaro** kyä′rō
light blue	**azzurro** ädzōō′rō
patterned	**fantasia** fäntäze′ä
pink	**rosa** *(inv)* rō′zä
purple	**lilla** *(inv)* lē′lä
red	**rosso** rō′sō
silver	**argentato** ärjentä′tō
solid *(color)*	**in tinta unita** ēn tēn′tä ōōnē′tä
striped	**a righe** ä rē′ge
white	**bianco** byän′kō
yellow	**giallo** jä′lō

INFO Stores in Italy are generally open from 8:30 or 9 a.m. to 1 p.m., and then again from 4:30 or 5:30 p.m. to 8 p.m. In many towns grocery stores are closed on Thursday afternoons, and hairdressers and clothing stores are closed on Mondays.

6

Stores

antique store	**il negozio di antiquariato** ēl negō'tsyō dē äntēkōō·äryä'tō
bakery	**la panetteria, il forno** lä päneterē'ä, ēl fōr'nō
barbershop	**il barbiere** ēl bärbye're
bookstore	**la libreria** lä lēbrerē'ä
butcher's	**la macelleria** lä mätshelerē'ä
clothing store	**il negozio di abbigliamento** ēl negō'tsyō dē äbēlyämen'tō
confectionery	**la pasticceria** lä pästētsherē'ä
dairy store	**la latteria** lä läterē'ä
department store	**il grande magazzino** ēl grän'de mägätsē'nō
drugstore	**la drogheria** lä drōgerē'ä
dry cleaner's	**la lavanderia a secco** lä lävänderē'ä ä se'kō
fish store	**la pescheria** lä peskerē'ä
florist's	**il floraio** ēl fyōra'yo
vegetable store	**il negozio di frutta e verdura** ēl negō'tsyō dē frōō'tä e verdōō'rä

143

grocery store	**il negozio di generi alimentari** ēl negō'tsyō dē jen'er'ē ālēmentä'rē
beauty shop	**il parrucchiere** ēl pärōōkye're
jewelry store	**la gioielleria** lä jōyelerē'ä
kiosk	**il chiosco** ēl kyō'skō
laundromat	**la lavanderia a gettone** lä lävänderē'ä ä jetō'ne
green market	**il mercato** ēl merkä'tō
music store	**il negozio di dischi** ēl negō'tsyō dē dē'skē
newsstand	**il giornalaio** ēl jōrnälä'yō
optician's	**l'ottico** lō'tēkō
perfume store	**la profumeria** lä prōfōōmerē'ä
camera store	**il negozio di articoli fotografici** ēl negō'tsyō dē ärtē'kōlē fōtōgrä'fētshē
shoe store	**il negozio di calzature** ēl negō'tsyō dē kältsätōō're
shoe-repair shop	**il calzolaio** ēl kältsōlä'yō
souvenir store	**il negozio di souvenir** ēl negō'tsyō dē sōōvenēr'
sporting-goods store	**il negozio di articoli sportivi** ēl negō'tsyō dē ärtē'kōlē spōrtē've
stationery store	**la cartoleria** lä kärtōlerē'ä
houseware store	**il negozio di casalinghi** ēl negō'tsyō dē käsälēn'gē
leather goods	**la pelletteria** lä peleterē'ä
supermarket	**il supermercato** ēl sōōpermerkä'tō
tobacconist's	**la tabaccheria** lä täbäkerē'ä

FOOD

What's that?	**Che cos'è quello?**	ke kōse'kōō·e'lō?
Could I have …, please?	**Per favore, mi dia …**	per fävō're, mē dē'ä …
100 grams of …	**un etto di …**	oon e'tō dē …
250 grams of …	**due etti e mezzo di …**	dōō'e e'tē e me'tsō dē …
a pound *(500 grams)* of …	**mezzo chilo di …**	me'tsō kē'lō dē …
a kilo of …	**un chilo di …**	ōōn kē'lō dē …
a slice of …	**una fetta di …**	ōō'nä fe'tä dē …
a piece of …	**un pezzo di …**	oon pe'tsō dē …
a serving of …	**una porzione di …**	ōō'nä pōrtsyō'ne dē …
half a liter of …	**mezzo litro di …**	me'tsō lē'trō dē …
A little *less/more*, please.	**Un po' di *meno/più*, per favore.**	ōōn pō dē *me'nō/pyōō*, per fävō're.
May I try some (of that), please?	**Lo posso assaggiare?**	lō pō'sō äsäjä're?

INFO Normal bread in central Italy (**il filone di pane** ēl fēlō'ne dē pä'ne) is made without salt. Recently most places also offer **pane integrale** pä'ne ēntegrä'lo (whole-wheat bread), **pane di segale** pä'ne de se'gäle (rye bread), and breads made of various kinds of grains (**pane ai cinque cereali** pä'ne ī tshēn'kōō·e tshere·ä'lē). **Panini all'olio** pänē'nē älō'lēō are small, soft rolls that are particularly good for sandwiches.

apple	**la mela** lä me'lä
– juice	**il succo di mele** ēl sōō'kō dē me'le
apricot	**l'albicocca** lälbēkō'kä
artichoke	**il carciofo** ēl kärtshō'fō
artificial sweetener	**il dolcificante** ēl dōlshēfēkän'te
avocado	**l'avocado** lävōkä'dō
baby food	**gli alimenti per la prima infanzia** lyē älēmen'tē per lä prē'mä ēnfän'tsyä
banana	**la banana** lä bänä'nä
basil	**il basilico** ēl bäzē'lēkō
beans	**i fagioli** ē fäjō'lē
broad –	**i fagioli bianchi** ē fäjō'lē byän'kē
green –	**i fagiolini** ē fäjōlē'nē
beef	**la carne di manzo** lä kär'ne dē män'tsō
beer	**la birra** lä bē'rä
non-alcoholic –	**la birra analcolica** lä bē'rä änälkō'lēkä
bread	**il pane** ēl pä'ne
– roll	**il panino** ēl pänē'nō
whole-wheat –	**il pane integrale** ēl pä'ne ēntegrä'le
broccoli	**i broccoli** ē brō'kōlē
butter	**il burro** ēl bōō'rō
cabbage	**il cavolo** ēl kä'vōlō
cake	**la torta** lä tōr'tä
canned goods	**lo scatolame** lō skätōlä'me
cheese	**il formaggio** ēl fōrmä'jō
cherries	**le ciliege** le tshēlye'je
chicken	**il pollo** ēl pō'lō

(hot) chocolate	**la cioccolata** lä tshōkōlä'tä
chop	**la cotoletta** lä kōtōle'tä
cocoa	**il cacao** ēl käkä'ō
coffee	**il caffè** ēl käfe'
cold cuts	**l'affettato** läfetä'tō
cookies	**i biscotti** ē bēskō'tē
corn	**il mais** ēl mä'ēs
cream	**la panna** lä pä'nä
cucumber	**il cetriolo** ēl tshetrē·ō'lō
cutlet	**la cotoletta** lä kōtōle'tä
dates	**i datteri** ē dä'terē
egg	**l'uovo,** *pl:* **le uova** lōō·ō'vō, *pl:* le ōō·ō'vä
eggplant	**la melanzana** lä meläntsä'nä
figs	**i fichi** ē fē'kē
fish	**il pesce** ēl pe'she
fruit	**la frutta** lä frōō'tä
garlic	**l'aglio** lä'lyō
grapes	**l'uva** lōō'vä
ground meat	**la carne macinata** lä kär'ne mätshēnä'tä
ham	**il prosciutto** ēl prōshōō'tō
boiled –	**il prosciutto cotto** ēl prōshōō'tō kō'tō
cured –	**il prosciutto crudo** ēl prōshōō'tō krōō'dō
honey	**il miele** ēl mye'le
jam	**la marmellata** lä märmelä'tä
juice	**il succo** ēl sōō'kō
ketchup	**il ketchup** ēl ke'tshäp
kiwi fruit	**il kiwi** ēl kē'uē
lamb	**la carne d'agnello** lä kär'ne dänye'lō

147

leek	**il porro** ēl pō'rō
lemon	**il limone** ēl lēmō'ne
lettuce	**la lattuga** lä lätōō'gä
margarine	**la margarina** lä märgärē'nä
mayonnaise	**la maionese** lä mäyōne'se
meat	**la carne** lä kär'ne
melon	**il melone** ēl melō'ne
milk	**il latte** ēl lä'te
skim –	**il latte scremato** ēl lä'te skremä'tō
mineral water	**l'acqua minerale** lä'kōō-ä mēnerä'le
nectarine	**la pescanoce** lä peskänō'tshe
nuts	**le noci** le nō'tshē
(rolled) oats	**i fiocchi d'avena** ē fyōkē däve'nä
oil	**l'olio** lō'lēō
olive	**l'oliva** lōlē'vä
– oil	**l'olio d'oliva** lō'lēō dōlē'vä
onion	**la cipolla** lä tshēpō'lä
orange	**l'arancia** lärän'tshä
– juice	**il succo d'arancia** ēl sōō'kō därän'tshä
oregano	**l'origano** lōrē'gänō
parsley	**il prezzemolo** ēl pretsemō'lō
pasta	**la pasta** lä pä'stä
pistachios	**i pistacchi** ē pēstä'kē
peach	**la pesca** lä pe'skä
peas	**i piselli** ē pēse'lē
pepper *(spice)*	**il pepe** ēl pe'pe
pepper *(vegetable)*	**il peperone** ēl peperō'ne
pineapple	**l'ananas** *m* länänäs'

148

pork	**la carne di maiale**	lä kär′ne dē mäyä′le
potatoes	**le patate**	le pätä′te
poultry	**il pollame**	ēl pōlä′me
raspberries	**i lamponi**	ē lämpō′nē
rice	**il riso**	ēl rē′sō
salami	**il salame**	ēl sälä′me
salt	**il sale**	ēl sä′le
sandwich	**il panino imbottito**	ēl pänē′nō ēmbōtē′tō
sausages	**le salsicce**	le sälsē′tshe
soft drink	**la gassosa**	lä gäsō′sä
spices	**le spezie**	le spe′tsye
steak	**la bistecca**	lä bēste′kä
strawberries	**le fragole**	le frä′gōle
sugar	**lo zucchero**	lō tsōō′kerō
tangerine	**la clementina**	lä klementē′nä
tea	**il tè**	ēl te
tomato	**il pomodoro**	ēl pōmōdō′rō
tuna	**il tonno**	ēl tō′nō
veal	**la carne di vitello**	lä kär′ne dē vēte′lō
vegetables	**la verdura**	lä verdōō′rä
vinegar	**l'aceto**	lätshe′tō
watermelon	**il cocomero**	ēl kōkō′merō
wine	**il vino**	ēl vē′nō
red –	**il vino rosso**	ēl vē′nō rō′so
white –	**il vino bianco**	ēl vē′nō byän′kō
yogurt	**lo yogurt**	lō yō′gōōrt
zucchini	**le zucchine**	le tsōōkē′ne
zwieback	**la fetta biscottata**	lä fe′tä bēskōtä′tä

SOUVENIRS

What's typical of this area?	**Che cosa c'è di tipico in questa zona?** ke kō'sä tshe dē tē'pēkō ēn kōō-e'stä dzō'nä?
Is this handmade?	**È fatto a mano?** e fä'tō ä mä'nō?
Is this *antique/genuine*?	**È *antico/autentico*?** e äntē'kō/outen'tēkō?

Souvenirs

arts and crafts	**l'artigianato artistico** lärtējänä'tō ärtē'stēkō
belt	**la cintura** lä tshēntōō'rä
Capodimonte porcelain	**la (porcellana) capodimonte** lä (pōrtshelä'nä) käpōdēmōn'te
ceramics	**la ceramica** lä tsherä'mēkä
copper pot	**il paiolo di rame** ēl päyō'lō dē rä'me
crafts	**l'artigianato** lärtējänä'tō
doily	**il centrino** ēl tshentrē'nō
genuine	**autentico** outen'tēkō
glass	**il vetro** ēl ve'trō
goblet	**il calice** ēl kä'lētshe
handbag	**la borsa** lä bōr'sä
handmade	**fatto a mano** fä'tō ä mä'nō
jewelry	**i gioielli** ē jōye'lē
lace	**il pizzo** ēl pē'tsō
leather	**la pelle** lä pe'le
plate *(for hanging on the wall)*	**il piatto murale** ēl pyä'tō mōōrä'le

150

rug	**il tappeto** ēl täpe'tō
shoulder bag	**la borsa a tracolla** lä bōr'sä ä träkō'lä
souvenir	**il souvenir** ēl sōōvenēr'
statuette	**la statuetta** lä stätōō·e'tä
straw hat	**il cappello di paglia** ēl käpe'lō dē pä'lyä
terracotta	**la terracotta** lä teräkō'tä
typical	**tipico** tē'pēkō

CLOTHES AND DRY CLEANER'S

I'm looking for ...	**Vorrei ...** vōre'ē ...
? Che taglia porta? ke tä'lyä pōr'tä?	What size are you?
I'm a size ...	**Ho la taglia ...** ō lä tä'lyä ...
Do you also have this in a size ... ?	**Ha anche la taglia ...?** ä än'ke lä tä'lyä ...?
Do you have this in another color?	**Ce l'ha anche di un altro colore?** tshe lä än'ke dē ōōn äl'trō kōlō're?
May I try this on?	**Lo posso provare?** lō pō'sō prōvä're?
Where is the mirror?	**Dov'è uno specchio?** dōve' ōō'nō spe'kyō?
What kind of material is this made of?	**Di che materiale è?** dē ke mäteryä'le e?
It doesn't fit.	**Non mi sta bene.** nōn mē stä be'ne.

It's too *big/small*.	**È troppo *grande/piccolo*.**
	e trô'pō *grän'de/pē'kōlō*.
This fits perfectly.	**Questo va bene.** kōō·e'stō vä be'ne.
I'd like this dry-cleaned.	**Vorrei far lavare a secco questo.**
	vōre'ē fär lävä're ä se'kō kōō·e'sto.
Can you get rid of this stain?	**Può togliere questa macchia?**
	pōō·ô' tōlye're kōō·e'stä mä'kyä?

Clothes and Dry Cleaners

belt	**la cintura** lä tshēntōō'rä
blazer	**il blazer** ēl ble'zä
blouse	**la camicetta** lä kämētshe'tä
bra	**il reggiseno** ēl rejēse'nō
cap	**il berretto** ēl bere'tō
coat	**il cappotto** ēl käpō'tō
collar	**il collo** ēl kō'lō
color	**il colore** ēl kōlō're
cotton	**il cotone** ēl kōtō'ne
dress	**il vestito** ēl vestē'tō
to dry-clean	**lavare a secco** lävä're ä se'kō
elegant	**elegante** elegän'te
to fit	**stare bene** stä're be'ne
gloves	**i guanti** ē gōō·än'tē
hat	**il cappello** ēl käpe'lō
jacket	**la giacca** lä jä'kä
jeans	**i jeans** ē jēnz
leather	**la pelle** lä pe'le

linen	**il lino** ēl lē'nō	
long	**lungo** lōōn'gō	
material	**il materiale** ēl mäteryä'le	**6**
nightgown	**la camicia da notte**	
	lä kämē'tshä dä nô'te	
pajamas	**il pigiama** ēl pējä'mä	
panties	**lo slip** lō slēp	
pants	**i pantaloni** ē päntälō'nē	
pantyhose	**il collant** ēl kôlän'	
permanent press	**non-stiro** nōn-stē'rō	
scarf *(silky)*	**il foulard** ēl fōōlär'	
scarf *(woolen)*	**la sciarpa** lä shär'pä	
shirt	**la camicia** lä kämē'tshä	
short	**corto** kôr'tō	
shorts	**gli shorts** lyē shōrts	
silk	**la seta** lä se'tä	
size	**la taglia** lä tä'lyä	
skirt	**la gonna** lä gô'nä	
sleeves	**le maniche** le mä'nēke	
long –	**le maniche lunghe** le mä'nēke lōōn'ge	
short –	**le maniche corte** le mä'nēke kôr'te	
socks	**i calzini** ē kältsē'nē	
stockings	**le calze** le käl'tse	
sun hat	**il cappello da sole** ēl käpe'lō dä sō'le	
sweater	**il maglione** ēl mälyō'ne	
sweatpants	**i pantaloni della tuta**	
	ē päntälō'nē de'lä tōō'tä	
sweatsuit	**la tuta da ginnastica**	
	lä tōō'tä dä jēnä'stēkä	

153

T-shirt	**la maglietta** lä mälye'tä
terry cloth	**la spugna** lä spōō'nyä
tie	**la cravatta** lä krävä'tä
to try on	**provare** prōvä're
underpants	**le mutande** le mōōtän'de
Windbreaker®	**la giacca a vento** lä jä'kä ä ven'tō
wool	**la lana** lä lä'nä

➡ *see also: Word list General Vocabulary (p. 141),*
  Word list Colors and Patterns (p. 142)

SHOES

I'd like a pair of ... **Vorrei un paio di ...**
vōre'ē ōōn pä'yō dē ...

? Che numero di scarpe ha?
  ke nōō'merō dē skär'pe ä?   What is your shoe
                                  size?

My size is ... **Ho il numero ...** ō ēl nōō'merō ...

The heel is too **Il tacco è troppo *alto/basso*.**
high/low for me. ēl tä'kō e trō'pō *äl'tō/bä'sō.*

They're too **Sono troppo *grandi/piccole.***
big/small. sō'nō trō'pō grän'dē/pē'kōle.

They're too tight **Mi fanno male qui.** mē fä'nō mä'le
around here. kōō-ē'.

154

Would you fix the heels, please?	**Mi rifaccia i tacchi, per favore.**
	mē rēfä'tshä ē tä'kē, per fävō're.
Could you re-sole the shoes, please?	**Me le può risuolare, per favore?**
	me le pōō·ō' rēsōō·ōlä're, per fävō're?

Shoes

boots	**gli stivali** lyē stēvä'lē
thongs	**le scarpette da bagno**
	le skärpe'tē dä bä'nyō
heel	**il tacco** ēl tä'kō
hiking boots	**le scarpe da escursioni**
	le skär'pe dä eskōōrsyō'nē
leather	**il cuoio** ēl kōō·ō'yō
– sole	**la suola di cuoio** lä sōō·ō'lä dē kōō·ō'yō
mountain climbing boots	**gli scarponi da montagna**
	lyē skärpō'nē dä mōntä'nyä
pair	**il paio** ēl pä'yō
pumps	**le scarpe decolleté** le skärpe dekōlte'
rubber sole	**la suola di gomma** lä sōō·ō'lä dē gō'mä
sandals	**i sandali** ē sändä'lē
shoe polish	**il lucido da scarpe**
	ēl lōō'tshēdō dä skär'pe
shoelaces	**i lacci per le scarpe**
	ē lä'tshe per le skär'pe
shoes	**le scarpe** le skär'pe
size	**il numero** ēl nōō'merō
sneakers	**le scarpe da ginnastica**
	le skär'pe dä jēnä'stēkä

155

WATCHES AND JEWELRY

My watch is fast/slow.

Il mio orologio va *avanti/indietro*. ēl mē'ō ōrōlō'jō vä ävän'tē/*ēndye'trō*.

I'm looking for a nice souvenir/present.

Vorrei un bel ricordino/regalo. vōre'ē ōōn bel rēkōrdē'nō/regä'lō.

? **Quanto vuole spendere?** kōō·an'tō vōō·ō'le spen'dere?

How much would you like to pay?

What's this made of?

Di che materiale è? dē ke mäteryä'le e?

Watches and Jewelry

alarm clock	**la sveglia**	lä sve'lyä
battery	**la pila**	lä pē'lä
bracelet	**il bracciale**	ēl brätshä'le
brass	**l'ottone**	lōtō'ne
brooch	**la spilla**	lä spē'la
chain	**la catenina**	lä kätenē'nä
clip-on earrings	**gli orecchini a clip**	lyē ōrekē'nē ä klēp
costume jewelry	**la bigiotteria**	lä bējōterē'ä
earrings	**gli orecchini**	lyē ōrekē'nē
gold	**l'oro**	lō'rō
gold-plated	**placcato in oro**	pläkä'tō ēn ō'rō
jewelry	**i gioielli**	ē jōye'lē
necklace	**la collana**	lä kōlä'nä
pendant	**il ciondolo**	ēl tshōn'dōlō
ring	**l'anello**	läne'lō

silver	**l'argento** lärjen'tō
silver-plated	**placcato in argento**
	pläkä'tō ēn ärjen'tō
watch	**l'orologio** lōrōlō'jō
–band	**il cinturino** ēl tshēntōōre'nō

PERSONAL HYGIENE AND HOUSEHOLD

INFO In Italy there is nothing exactly like the drug-stores in America. You will find some things in the **drogheria** drōgerē'ä. Otherwise you can purchase articles for personal hygiene and for infant care at the **farmacia** färmätshē'ä (pharmacy), and soaps and other cosmetic articles in the **profumeria** profōōmerē'ä (perfume store) or at the supermarket.

Personal Hygiene

aftershave	**il dopobarba** ēl dōpōbär'bä
baby bottle	**il biberon** ēl bēberōn!
– nipple	**la tettarella** lä tetäre'lä
baby oil	**l'olio emolliente** lō'lēō emōlyen'te
baby powder	**il borotalco** ēl bōrōtäl'kō
barrette	**il fermaglio per i capelli**
	ēl fermä'lyō per ē käpe'lē
bath and shower	**il gel per la doccia**
gel	ēl jel per lä dō'tshä
bib	**il bavaglino** ēl bävälyē'nō
blusher	**il fard** ēl färd

157

body lotion	**la lozione per il corpo**
	lä lōtsyō'ne per ēl kōr'pō
brush	**la spazzola** lä spä'tsōlä
cleansing cream	**il latte detergente** ēl lä'te deterjen'te
comb	**il pettine** ēl pe'tēne
condoms	**i profilattici, i preservativi**
	ē prōfēlä'tētshē, ē preservätē've
cotton	**il cotone idrofilo** ēl kōtō'ne ēdrō'fēlō
– pads	**i dischetti uso cosmetico**
	ē dēske'tē ōō'zō kōsme'tēkō
deodorant	**il deodorante** ēl de·ōdōrän'te
detergent	**il detersivo** ēl deterse'vō
diapers	**i pannolini** ē pänōle'nē
eye shadow	**l'ombretto** lōmbre'tō
fragrance-free	**non profumato** nōn prōfōōmä'tō
hair drier	**l'asciugacapelli** *m* läshōōgäkäpe'lē
hair-styling gel	**il gel per capelli** ēl jel per käpe'lē
hair-styling mousse	**la schiuma (fissante)**
	lä skyōō'mä (fēsän'te)
hairband	**l'elastico per i capelli**
	lelä'stēkō per ē käpe'lē
hairspray	**la lacca** lä lä'kä
handcream	**la crema per le mani**
	lä kre'mä per le mä'nē
handkerchief	**il fazzoletto** ēl fatsōle'tō
lip balm	**il burro cacao** ēl bōō'rō käkä'ō
lipstick	**il rossetto** ēl rōse'tō
mascara	**il mascara** ēl mäskä'rä
mirror	**lo specchio** lō spe'kyō

158

mosquito repellent	**il fornellino antizanzare**
	ēl förnelē'nō äntēdzändzä're
nail file	**la limetta per le unghie**
	lä lēme'tä per le ōōn'gye
nail polish	**lo smalto per le unghie**
	lō zmäl'tō per le ōōn'gye
– remover	**il solvente per lo smalto**
	ēl sōlven'te per lō zmäl'tō
nail scissors	**le forbici per le unghie**
	le fōr'bētshē per le ōōn'gye
pacifier	**il succhietto** ēl sōōkye'tō
paper towels	**gli asciugamani usa e getta**
	lyē äshōōgämä'nē ōō'zä e je'tä
perfume	**il profumo** ēl prōfōō'mō
pH-balanced	**pH-neutro** pē-ä'kä-ne'ōōtrō
plaster	**il cerotto** ēl tsherō'tō
powder	**la cipria** lä tshēp'rē-ä
razor	**il rasoio** ēl räsō'yō
– blade	**la lametta** lä läme'tä
sanitary napkins	**gli assorbenti igienici**
	lyē äsörben'tē ēje'nētshē
shampoo	**lo shampoo** lō shäm'pō
skin cream	**la crema per la pelle**
	lä kre'mä per lä pe'le
– for dry skin	**la crema per pelli secche**
	lä kre'mä per pe'lē se'ke
– for oily skin	**la crema per pelli grasse**
	lä kre'mä per pe'lē grä'se
soap	**la saponetta** lä säpōne'tä

6

159

SPF (sun pro- tection factor)	**il fattore di protezione** ĕl fätö're dē prōtĕtsēō'ne
suntan cream	**la crema solare** lä kre'mä sōlä're
suntan gel	**il gel solare** ĕl jel sōlä're
suntan lotion	**il latte solare** ĕl lä'te sōlä're
tampons	**i tamponi** ē tämpō'nē
tissues	**i fazzoletti da strucco, – di carta** ē fätsōle'tē dä strōō'kō dē kär'tä
toilet paper	**la carta igienica** lä kär'tä ēje'nēkä
toothbrush	**lo spazzolino da denti** lō spätsōlē'nō dä den'tē
toothpaste	**il dentifricio** ĕl dentēfrē'tshō
towel	**l'asciugamano** läshōōgämä'nō
tweezers	**le pinzette** le pēntse'tē
washcloth	**il guanto di spugna** ĕl gōō·än'tō dē spōō'nyä

Household

adapter	**l'adattatore** *m* lädätätō're
alarm clock	**la sveglia** lä zve'lyä
aluminum foil	**il foglio di alluminio** ĕl fō'lyō dē älōōmē'nyō
battery	**la pila** lä pē'lä
bottle opener	**l'apribottiglie** *m* läprēbōtē'lye
broom	**la scopa** lä skō'pä
bucket	**il secchio** ĕl se'kyō
can opener	**l'apriscatole** *m* läprēskä'tōle
candle	**la candela** lä kände'lä

160

charcoal	**la carbonella** lä kärbōne'lä
cleaning products	**il detersivo** ēl detersē'vō
clothes line	**il filo per stendere i panni** ēl fē'lō per sten'dere ē pä'nē
clothes pins	**le mollette (per i panni)** le mōle'te (per ē pä'nē)
corkscrew	**il cavatappi** ēl kävätä'pē
cup	**la tazza** lä tä'tsä
paper –	**il bicchiere di carta** ēl bēkye're dē kär'tä
detergent	**il detersivo** ēl detersē'vō
dish-washing liquid	**il detersivo per le stoviglie** ēl detersē'vō per le stōve'lye
dishcloth	**lo strofinaccio** lō strōfēnä'tshō
extension cord	**la prolunga** lä prōlōōn'gä
flashlight	**la lampada tascabile** lä läm'pädä täskä'bēle
fork	**la forchetta** lä fōrke'tä
gas cartridge	**la cartuccia per il fornellino a gas** lä kärtōō'tshä per ēl fōrnelē'nō ä gäs
glass	**il bicchiere** ēl bēkye're
grill	**il grill** ēl grēl
knife	**il coltello** ēl kōlte'lō
light bulb	**la lampadina** lä lämpädē'nä
lighter	**l'accendino** lätshendē'nō
matches	**i fiammiferi** ē fyämē'ferē
mosquito net	**la zanzariera** lä dzändzärye'rä
napkins	**i tovaglioli** ē tōvälyō'lē
pan	**la padella** lä päde'lä

plastic cutlery	**le posate di plastica**
	lē pō̄sa'te de plä'stēkä
plate	**il piatto** ēl pyä'tō
paper –	**i piatti di carta** ē pyä'tē dē kär'tä
pocket knife	**il coltello tascabile**
	ēl kōlte'lō täskä'bēle
pot	**la pentola** lä pen'tōlä
safety pin	**lo spillo da balia** lō spē'lō dä bä'lyä
scissors	**le forbici** lē fōr'bētshē
scrubbing brush	**lo spazzolone** lō spätsōlō'ne
sewing needle	**l'ago** lä'gō
solid fire lighter	**l'accendifuoco** lätshendēfōō·ō'kō
spoon	**il cucchiaio** ēl kōōkyä'yō
string	**lo spago** lō spä'gō
thread	**il filo da cucito** ēl fē'lō dä kōōtshē'tō
toothpick	**lo stuzzicadenti** lō stōōtsēkäden'tē

AT THE OPTICIAN'S

My glasses are broken.	**Mi si sono rotti gli occhiali.** mē sē sō'nō rō'tē lyē ōkyä'lē.
Can you fix this?	**Me lo può aggiustare?** me lō pōō·ō' äjōōstä're?
I'm *nearsighted/ farsighted*.	**Sono *miope/presbite*.** sō'nō mē'ōpe/prez'bēte.

162

I'd like a pair of *sunglasses/prescription sunglasses*.	**Vorrei un paio di occhiali *da sole/da vista con filtro solare*.** vôre'ē ōōn pä'yō dē ōkyä'lē dä sō'le/dä vē'stä kôn fēl'trō sōlä're.	

I've *lost/broken* a contact lens.

Ho perso/Mi si è rotta una lente a contatto. ō per'sō/mē sē e rō'tä ōō'nä len'te ä kôntä'tō.

I need some *rinsing/cleaning* solution for *hard/soft* contact lenses.

Ho bisogno di una soluzione *per la conservazione/detergente* per lenti a contatto *rigide/morbide*. ō bēzō'nyō dē ōō'nä sōlōōtsyō'ne *per lä kōnservätsēō'ne/deterjen'te* per len'tē ä kôntä'tō rē'jēde/môr'bēde.

AT THE HAIRDRESSER'S

I'd like to make an appointment for ...	**Vorrei un appuntamento per ...** vôre'ē ōōn äpōōntämen'tō per ...	
? **Che cosa deve fare?** ke kô'sä de've fä're?		What would you like to have done?
Just a trim, please.	**Soltanto il taglio.** sôltän'tō ēl tä'lyō.	
I'd like it washed, cut and blow dried, please.	**Taglio, shampoo e fon, per favore.** tä'lyō, shäm'pō e fōn, per fävō're.	
? **Come vuole tagliarli?** kō'me vōō∙ō'le tälyär'lē?		How do you want it cut?

163

I'd like …	**Vorrei …** vōre'ē
a perm.	**una permanente.** ōō'nä permänen'te.
some highlights put in.	**farmi le mèche.** fär'mē le mesh.
to have a color rinse.	**dei riflessi.** de'ē rēfle'sē.

Not too short, please. **Non troppo corti, per favore.**
nōn trō'pō kōr'tē, per fävō're.

A little shorter, please. **Un po' più corti, per favore.**
ōōn pō pyōō kōr'tē, per fävō're.

Could you make the … a bit shorter, please? **Li sfoltisca un po' …, per favore.**
lē sfōltē'skä ōōn pō …, per fävō're.

back	**dietro** dye'trō
front	**davanti** dävän'tē
sides	**ai lati** ī lä'tē
top	**sopra** sō'prä

Part it on the *left/right*, please. **Faccia la riga a *sinistra/destra*, per favore.** fä'tshä lä rē'gä ä *sēnēs'trä/des'trä*, per fävō're.

Please trim my beard. **Mi tagli la barba, per favore.**
mē tä'lyē lä bär'bä, per fävō're.

Please give me a shave. **La barba, per favore.**
lä bär'bä, per fävō're.

164

bangs	**la frangetta** lä fränje'tä
beard	**la barba** lä bär'bä
black	**nero** ne'rō
blond(e)	**biondo** byōn'dō
to blow-dry	**asciugare con il fon** äshōōgä're kōn ĕl fōn
chestnut (brown)	**castano** kästä'nō
color rinse	**il riflessante** ĕl rēflesän'te
to cut	**tagliare** tälyä're
dandruff	**la forfora** lä fōr'fōrä
to dye	**tingere** tēn'jere
hair	**i capelli** ē käpe'lē
– cut	**il taglio** ĕl tä'lyō
dry –	**i capelli secchi** ē käpe'lē se'kē
oily –	**i capelli grassi** ē käpe'lē grä'sē
– spray	**la lacca** lä lä'kä
– style	**la pettinatura** lä petēnätōō'rä
highlights	**le mèche** le mesh
moustache	**i baffi** ē bä'fē
part *(in hair)*	**la riga** lä rē'gä
perm	**la permanente** lä permänen'te
razor cut	**il taglio con il rasoio** ĕl tä'lyō kōn ĕl räsō'yō
to set in curlers	**mettere in piega** me'tere ēn pve'gä
shampoo	**lo shampoo** lō shäm'pō
to shave	**fare la barba** fä're lä bär'ba
to wash	**lavare** lävä're

PHOTO AND VIDEO

I'd like …

a roll of film for
this camera.

a *color/black-and-white* film.

a slide film.

a *24/36* exposure
film.

a …ASA film.

a VHS video
cassette.

I'd like some
batteries for this
camera.

Could you please put
the film in for me?

I'd like to get this film
developed.

Vorrei … vōre′ē

**una pellicola per questa macchina
fotografica.** ōō′na pelē′kōla per
kōō·e′stä mä′kēna fōtōgrä′fēkä.

**una pellicola *a colori/in bianco e
nero.*** ōō′nä pelē′kōlä *ä kōlō′rē/ēn
byän′kō e ne′rō.*

una pellicola per diapositive.
ōō′nä pelē′kōlä per dē·äpōzētē′ve.

**una pellicola da *ventiquattro/
trentasei pose.*** ōō′nä pelē′kōlä dä
ventēkōō·ä′trō/trentäse′ē pō′se.

una pellicola da … ASA.
ōō′nä pelē′kōlä dä … ä′sä.

una videocassetta VHS.
ōō′nä vēde·ōkäse′tä vōō·ä′kä-e′se.

**Vorrei delle pile per questa macchina
fotografica.** vōre′ē de′le pē′le per
kōō·e′stä mä′kēna fōtōgrä′fēkä.

**Mi potrebbe inserire la pellicola, per
favore?** mē pōtre′be ēnsere′re lä
pelē′kōlä, per fävō′re?

Vorrei far sviluppare questo rullino.
vōre′ē fär zvēlōōpä′re kōō·e′stō rōōlē′nō.

166

Just develop the negatives, please.	**Soltanto le negative, per favore.** sŏltän'tŏ le negätē've, per fävō're.

I'd like a ... x ... picture from each negative, please.	**Una stampa di ogni negativa, formato ... per ..., per favore.** ōō'na stäm'pä dē ō'nyē negätē'vä, formä'tŏ ... per ..., per fävō're.

? Lucido od opaco? lōō'tshēdŏ ōd ōpä'kŏ?	Glossy or silk finish?

When will the pictures be ready?	**Quando saranno pronte le foto?** kōō·än'dŏ särä'nŏ prōn'te le fō'tŏ?

Could you repair my camera?	**Mi potrebbe riparare la macchina fotografica?** mē pōtre'be rēpärä're lä mä'kēnä fŏtŏgrä'fēkä?

The film doesn't wind forward.	**La pellicola non scorre.** lä pelē'kŏlä nŏn skŏ're.

The *shutter release/ flash* doesn't work.	**Lo scatto/Il flash non funziona.** lŏ skä'tŏ/ēl flesh nŏn fōōntsyō'nä.

I'd like to have passport photos taken.	**Vorrei farmi delle foto formato tessera.** vōre'ē fär'mē de'le fō'tŏ formä'tŏ te'serä.

Do you have any ... by ...?	**Avete ... di ...?** äve'te ... dē ...?

CD's	**dei compact disc** de'ē kōm'päkt dēsk
cassettes	**delle cassette** de'lē käse'te
records	**dei dischi** de'ē dē'skē

167

| Do you have the latest cassette by … | **Vorrei l'ultima cassetta di …** vōre'ē lōōl'tēmä käse'tä dē … |

I'm interested in folk music. What would you recommend?

Mi interessa molto la musica tradizio-nale. Potrebbe consigliarmi qualcosa? mē ēntere'sä mōl'tō lä mōō'zēkä trädētsyōnä'le. pōtre'be kōnsēlyär'mē kōō-älkō'sä?

Photo and Video

automatic shutter	**l'autoscatto** loutōskä'tō
battery	**la pila** lä pē'lä
camera	**la macchina fotografica** lä mä'kēnä fōtōgrä'fēkä
cassette	**la cassetta** lä käse'tä
CD	**il compact disc** ēl kōm'päkt dēsk
to develop	**sviluppare** zvēlōōpä're
to expose	**esporre** espō're
film	**la pellicola** lä pelē'kōlä
black-and-white –	**la pellicola in bianco e nero** lä pelē'kōlä ēn byän'kō e ne'rō
color –	**la pellicola a colori** lä pelē'kōlä ä kōlō'rē
slide –	**la pellicola per diapositive** lä pelē'kōlä per dē-äpōzētē've
to film	**filmare** fēlmä're
flash	**il flash** ēl flesh
lens	**l'obiettivo** lōbyetē'vō
light meter	**l'esposimetro** lespōzēm'etrō
movie camera	**la cinepresa** lä tshēnepre'sä

music	**la musica** lä mōō'zēkä
negative	**il negativo** ēl negätē'vō
picture	**la foto** lä fō'tō
radio	**la radio** lä rä'dyō
record *(LP)*	**il disco** ēl dē'skō
shutter	**lo scatto** lō skä'tō
slide	**la diapositiva** lä dē·äpōzētē'vä
UV filter	**il filtro UV** ēl fē'ltrō ōō·vē'
VHS	**VHS** vōō·ä'kä·e'se
video-8	**il video-8** ēl vē'de·ō·ō'tō
videocamera	**la videocamera** lä vēde·ōkä'merä
videocassette	**la videocassetta** lä vēde·ōkäse'tä
Walkman®	**il Walkman®** ēl vōōk'men
wide-angle lens	**il grandangolare** ēl grändän·gōlä're
zoom lens	**il teleobiettivo** ēl tele·ōbyetē'vō

6

READING AND WRITING

I'd like …

an *American/ English* newspaper.

an *American/ English* magazine

a map of the area.

Vorrei … võre'ē …

un giornale *americano/inglese.*
ōōn jōrnä'le ämerēkä'nō/ēn·gle'se.

una rivista *americana/inglese.*
ōō'nä rēvē'stä ämerēkä'nä/en·gle'se.

una cartina di questa zona.
ōō'nä kärtē'nä dē kōō·e'stä dzō'nä.

Do you have a more current issue?	**Ha anche un giornale più recente?** ä än'ke ōōn jōrnä'le pyōō retshen'te?
Do you have any books in English?	**Avete anche dei libri in inglese?** äve'te än'ke de'ē lē'brē ēn ēn·gle'se?
Do you have stamps?	**Si possono comprare anche i francobolli qui?** sē pō'sōnō kōmprä're än'ke ē fränkōbō'lē kōō·ē'?

Reading and Writing

adhesive tape	**il nastro adesivo** ēl näs'trō ädeze'vō
ball-point pen	**la penna a sfera** lä pe'nä ä sfe'rä
board game	**il gioco di società** ēl jō'kō dē sōtsh·etä'
book	**il libro** ēl lē'brō
color pencil	**la matita colorata** lä mätē'tä kōlōrä'tä
coloring book	**l'album** *m* **da colorare** läl'bōōm dä kōlōrä're
cookbook	**il libro di cucina** ēl lē'brō dē kōōtshē'nä
dictionary	**il dizionario** ēl dētsyōnär'yō
drawing pad	**l'album** *m* **da dissegno** läl'bōōm dä dēse'nyō
envelope	**la busta** lä bōō·stä
eraser	**la gomma per cancellare** lä gō'mä per käntshelä're
felt-tip pen	**il pennarello** ēl penäre'lō
glue	**la colla** lä kō'lä
ink cartridges	**le cartucce per la stilografica** le kärtōō'tshe per lä stēlōgrä'fēkä
magazine	**la rivista** lä rēvē'sta

map	**la carta** lä kär'tä
– of bicycle routes	**la carta dei percorsi ciclabili** lä kär'tä de'ē perkōr'sē tshēklä'bēlē
city –	**la cartina della città** lä kärtē'nä de'lä tshētä'
– of hiking trails	**la carta dei percorsi escursionistici** lä kär'tä de'ē perkōr'sē eskōōrsyōnē'stētshē
newspaper	**il giornale (quotidiano)** ēl jōrnä'le (kōō·ōtēdyä'nō)
note pad	**il bloc-notes** ēl blōk-nō'tes
novel	**il romanzo** ēl rōmän'tsō
detective –	**il giallo** ēl jä'lō
paper	**la carta** lä kär'tä
airmail –	**la carta da lettere per posta aerea** lä kär'tä dä le'tere per pō'stä ä·e're·ä
pencil	**la matita** lä mätē'tä
– sharpener	**il temperamatite** ēl temperämätē'te
picture book	**il libro illustrato** ēl le'brō ēlōōsträ'tō
playing cards	**le carte da gioco** le kär'te dä jō'kō
postcard	**la cartolina** lä kärtōlē'nä
road map	**la carta stradale** lä kär'tä strädä'le
stamp	**il francobollo** ēl fränkōbō'lō
travel guide	**la guida** lä gōō·ē'dä
wrapping paper	**la carta da regalo** lä kär'tä dä regä'lō
writing paper	**la carta da lettere** lä kär'tä dä le'tere

6

AT THE TOBACCONIST'S

Do you have any
American cigarettes?

Ha sigarette americane?
ä sēgäre'te ämerēkä'ne?

A pack of ...,
filtered/unfiltered
cigarettes, please.

Un pacchetto di sigarette *con/senza*
filtro, per favore. ōōn päke'tō dē
sēgäre'te *kôn/sen'tsä* fēl'trō, per fävō're.

INFO You can purchase cigarettes in the **tabaccheria**
täbäkerē'ä (tobacconist's) and in bars desig-
nated as a **bar tabaccheria** bär täbäkerē'ä by a blue sign with a
white "T." You can also get stamps in either of these.

A pack/A carton
of ..., please.

Un pacchetto/Una stecca di ..., per
favore. ōōn päke'tō/ōō'nä ste'kä dē ...,
per fävō're.

A package of ...
pipe/cigarette
tobacco, please.

Un pacchetto di tabacco *da pipa/per*
sigarette, per favore. ōōn päke'tō dē
täbä'kō *dä pē'pä/per sēgäre'te*, per
fävō're.

Could I have *a box of*
matches/a lighter,
please?

Una scatola di fiammiferi/Un
accendino, per favore. ōō'nä skä'tōlä dē
fyämē'ferē/ōōn ätshende'nō, per fävō're.

Entertainment and Sports

SWIMMING AND WATER SPORTS

At the Beach

Is there a beach nearby?	**C'è una spiaggia qui vicino?** tshe ōō'nä spyä'jä kōō-ē' vētshē'no?
How do you get to the beach?	**Come si arriva alla spiaggia?** kō'me sē äre'vä ä'lä spyä'jä?

INFO In Italy there are **spiagge private** spyä'je prēvä'te (private beaches) which you may not use because they belong to private citizens or hotels. The **stabilimenti balneari** stäbēlēmen'tē bälne-ä'rē are sections of beach that are watched over and cleaned privately or by companies. If you wish to visit one of these beaches, you are required to rent a space with an umbrella and a lounge chair. Only the **spiagge libere** spyä'je lē'bere (public beaches) may be used at no cost.

Is there any shade there?	**C'è un po' d'ombra?** tshē ōōn pō dōm'brä?
How *deep/warm* is the water?	**Quant'è *alta/calda* l'acqua?** kōō-änte' äl'tä/käl'dä lä'kōō-ä?
Are there strong currents here?	**Ci sono delle correnti?** tshē sō'nō de'le kōren'tē?
Is it dangerous for children?	**È pericoloso per i bambini?** e perēkōlō'sō per ē bämbē'nē?

174

Are there jellyfish around here?	**Ci sono meduse?** tshē sō'nō medōō'ze?
Where can I rent ...?	**Dove si può noleggiare ...?** dō've sē pōō·ō' nōlejä're ...?
I'd like to rent a *lounge chair/beach umbrella*.	**Vorrei noleggiare *una sedia a sdraio/un ombrellone*.** vōre'ē nōlejä're ōō'nä se'dyä ä zdrä'yō/ōōn ōmbrelō'ne.
I'd like to go waterskiing.	**Vorrei fare dello sci acquatico.** vōre'ē fä're de'lō shē äkōō·ä'tēkō.
I'd like to take *scuba diving/windsurfing* lessons.	**Vorrei fare un corso di *nuoto subacqueo/surf*.** vōre'ē fä're ōōn kōr'sō dē *nōō·ō'tō sōōbäkōō·e'ō/serf*.
Would you keep an eye on my things for a moment, please?	**Per favore, starebbe attento alle mie cose per un attimo?** per fävō're, stäre'be äten'tō ä'le mē'e kō'se per ōōn ä'tēmō?

At the Swimming Pool

Is there an *indoor/outdoor* pool nearby?	**C'è una piscina *all'aperto/coperta* qui vicino?** tshe ōō'nä pēshē'nä *äläper'tō/kōper'tä* kōō·ē vētshē'nō?
How much does it cost to get in?	**Quanto costa il biglietto d'ingresso?** kōō·än'tō kō'stä ēl bēlye'tō dēngre'sō?
What coins do I need for the *lockers/hair-dryers*?	**Che monete ci vogliono per *gli armadletti/l'asciugacapelli*?** ke mōne'te tshē vōl'yōnō per *lyē ärmädye'tē/läshōōgäkäpe'lē*?

175

Is there also a sauna here?	**C'è anche la sauna?** tshe än'ke lä sou'nä?
I'd like to rent ...	**Vorrei noleggiare ...** võre'ē nōlejä're ...
a bathing cap.	**una cuffia.** ōō'nä kōō'fyä.
a towel.	**un asciugamano.** ōōn äshōōgämä'nō.
some water wings.	**dei bracciali salvagente.** de'ē brätshä'lē sälväjen'te.
Where's the *lifeguard/first-aid station*?	**Dov'è il *bagnino/posto di pronto soccorso*?** dōve' ēl bänyē'no/pō'stō dē prōn'tō sōkōr'sō?

Swimming and Water Sports

air mattress	**il materassino pneumatico** ēl mäteräsē'nō pnē-ōōmä'tēkō
bathing cap	**la cuffia** lä kōō'fyä
bathing suit	**il costume da bagno** ēl kōstōō'me dä bä'nyō
beach	**la spiaggia** lä spyä'jä
– umbrella	**l'ombrellone** lōmbrelō'ne
bikini	**il bikini** ēl bēkē'nē
boat	**la barca** lä bär'kä
– rental	**il noleggio di barche** ēl nōle'jō dē bär'ke
calm	**calmo** käl'mō
changing room	**la cabina** lä käbē'nä
current	**la corrente** lä kōren'te
dangerous	**pericoloso** perēkōlō'sō
deckchair	**la sedia a sdraio** lä se'dyä ä zdrä'yō

176

diving board	**il trampolino** ēl trämpōlē'nō
diving gear	**l'equipaggiamento da sub** lekōō·ēpäjämen'tō dä sōōb
to go fishing	**pescare** peskä're
fishing boat	**il peschereccio** ēl peskere'tshō
flippers	**le pinne** le pē'ne
heated spa	**il bagno termale** ēl bä'nyō termä'le
inflatable boat	**il canotto pneumatico** ēl käno'tō pne·ōōmä'tēkō
jellyfish	**la medusa** lä medōō'zä
lifesaver	**il salvagente** ēl sälväjen'te
motorboat	**il motoscafo** ēl mōtōskä'fō
non-swimmer	**i non nuotatori** ē nōn nōō·ōtätō'rē
nudist beach	**la spiaggia per nudisti** lä spyä'jä per nōōdē'stē
outdoor pool	**la piscina all'aperto** lä pēshē'nä äläper'tō
pedal boat	**il pattino a pedali** ēl pätē'nō ä pedä'lē
rocks *(large)*	**gli scogli** *m/pl* lye skōlyē
rough *(sea)*	**mosso** mō'sō
rowboat	**la barca a remi** lä bär'kä ä re'mē
to go sailing	**praticare la vela** prätēkä're lä ve'lä
sailboat	**la barca a vela** lä bär'kä ä ve'lä
sand	**la sabbia** lä sä'byä
sandy beach	**la spiaggia con la sabbia** lä spyä'jä kōn lä sä'byä
sauna	**la sauna** lä sou'nä
to go scuba diving	**fare nuoto subacqueo** fä're nōō·ō'tō subä'kōō·ō
sea	**il mare** ēl mä're

7

177

– urchin	**il riccio di mare** ēl rē'tshō dē mä're	
shade	**l'ombra** lōm'brä	
shells	**le conchiglie** le kōnkē'lye	
shower	**la doccia** lä dō'tshä	
snorkel	**il respiratore** ēl respērätō're	
storm warning	**il segnale di tempesta**	
	ēl senyä'le dē tempe'stä	
surfboard	**la tavola da surf** lä tä'vōlä dä serf	
to go swimming	**nuotare** nōō-ōtä're	
(as a sport)		
to go swimming	**fare il bagno** fä're ēl bä'nyō	
(for pleasure)		
swimming pool	**la piscina** lä pēshē'nä	
swimming trunks	**il costume da bagno** ēl kōstōō'me dä bä'nyō	
tide	**la marea** lä märe'ä	
high –	**l'alta marea** läl'tä märe'ä	
low –	**la bassa marea** lä bä'sä märe'ä	
towel	**l'asciugamano** läshōōgämä'nō	
water	**l'acqua** lä'kōō-ä	
– polo	**la pallanuoto** lä pälänōō-ō'tō	
– skiing	**lo sci acquatico** lō shē äkōō-ä'tēkō	
– wings	**i bracciali salvagente**	
	ē brätshä'lē sälväjen'te	
wave	**l'onda** lōn'dä	
wet suit	**la tuta subacquea** lä tōō'tä sōōbä'kōō-e-ä	
wicker beach chair	**la poltroncina da spiaggia**	
	lä pōltrōntshē'nä dä spyä'jä	
wind-surfing school	**la scuola di surf** lä skōō-ō'lä dä serf	

MOUNTAINEERING

I'd like to take a … hour hike.

Vorrei fare un'escursione di … ore.
võre'ē fä're ōōneskōōrsyō'ne dē … ō're.

I'd like to *go to/climb* …

Vorrei andare *a/su* …
võre'ē ändä're ä/sōō …

Can you recommend *an easy/a moderately difficult* hiking trail?

Mi può consigliare un percorso *piuttosto facile/di media difficoltà?*
mē pōō·ò' kõnsēlyä're ōōn perkōr'sō pyōōt'stō fä'tshēle/dē me'dyä dēfēkōltä'?

Approximately how long will it take?

Quanto tempo ci vuole all'incirca?
kōō·än'tō tem'pō tshē vōō·ò'le älentshēr'kä?

Is the path *well marked/secure?*

L'itinerario è ben *indicato/sicuro?*
lētēnerär'yō e ben ēndēkä'tō/sēkōō'rō?

Is there anywhere we can get something to eat along the way?

C'è un luogo di ristoro lungo il percorso? tshe ōōn lōō·ò'gō dē rēstō'rō lōōn'gō ēl perkōr'sō?

Are there guided tours?

Ci sono escursioni guidate?
tshē sō'nō eskōōrsyō'nē gōō·ēdä'te?

When does the *next/last* cable car go *up/come down?*

A che ora parte *la prossima/l'ultima* funivia per *salire/scendere?* ä ke ō'rä pär'te lä prò'sēmä/lōōl'tēmä fōōnōvō'ä per säle're/shen'dere?

Is this the right way to …?	**Siamo sulla strada giusta per …?**
	syä'mō sōō'lä strä'dä jōō'stä per …?
How much farther is it to …?	**Quanto manca per arrivare a …?**
	kōō·än'tō män'kä per ärēvä're ä …?
I'm not afraid of heights.	**Non soffro di vertigini.**
	nōn sō'frō dē vertē'jēnē

Mountaineering

cable car	**la funivia** lä fōōnēvē'ä
chair lift	**la seggiovia** lä sejōve'ä
hike	**l'escursione** f leskōōrsyō'ne
to go hiking	**fare escursioni** fä're eskōōrsyō'nē
hiking boots	**le scarpe da escursione**
	le skär'pe dä eskōōrsyō'ne
hiking map	**la carta dei sentieri**
	lä kär'tä de'ē sentye're̅
hiking trail	**il sentiero** ēl sentye'rō
hut	**il rifugio** ēl rēfōō'jō
mountain	**la montagna** lä mōntä'nyä
– climbing	**l'alpinismo** lälpēnēz'mō
– guide	**la guida alpina** lä gōō·ē'dä älpē'nä
mountain-climbing boots	**gli scarponi da montagna**
	lyē skärpō'nē dä mōntä'nyä
provisions	**le provviste** f/pl le prōvē'ste
ravine	**la gola** lä gō'lä
rope	**la corda** lä kōr'dä

SKIING

I'd like to …

Vorrei … vōrè'ē …

   enroll my
   son/daughter for
   skiing lessons.

   iscrivere *mio figlio/mia figlia* al
   corso di sci. ēskrē'vere *mē'ō*
   fē'lyō/mē'ä fē'lyä äl kôr'sō dē shē.

   take a skiing
   course.

   fare un corso di sci.
   fä're ōōn kôr'sō dē shē.

   have a private in-
   structor.

   prendere un maestro di sci.
   pren'dere ōōn mä·estrō dē she.

I'd like to rent …

Vorrei noleggiare …
vōre'ē nōlejä're …

   cross-country
   skis.

   un paio di sci da fondo.
   ōōn pä'yō dē shē dä fôn'dō.

   cross-country
   skiing boots,
   size …

   un paio di scarpette da sci di fondo
   numero … ōōn pä'yō dē skärpe'te
   dä'shē dē fôn'dō nōō'merō …

   downhill skis.

   un paio di sci da discesa.
   ōōn pä'yō dē shē dä dēshe'sä.

   downhill skiing
   boots, size …

   un paio di scarponi da sci numero …
   ōōn pä'yō dē skärpō'nē dä shē
   nōō'merō …

   a snowboard.

   uno snowboard. ōō'nō snō'bōrd.

   ice skates, size …

   un paio di pattini numero …
   oon pa'yō dē pä'tēne nōō'merō …

   a sled.

   una slitta. ōō'nä slē'tä.

I'm …	**Sono …** sō'nō …
a beginner.	♂ **un principiante** / ♀ **una principiante.** ♂ ōōn prēntshēpyän'te/ ♀ ōō'nä prēntshēpyän'te.
an average skiier.	**uno sciatore piuttosto mediocre.** ōōn'nō shē·äto're pyōōto'stō medyö'kre.
a good skiier.	**un bravo sciatore.** ōōn brä'vō shē·äto're.
I'd like a lift pass for …	**Vorrei uno ski-pass per …** vōre'ē ōō'nō skē'päs per …
a half-day.	**mezza giornata.** me'tsä jörnä'tä.
a day.	**un giorno.** ōōn jör'nō.
two days.	**due giorni.** dōō'e jör'nē.
a week.	**una settimana.** ōō'nä setēmä'nä.

> ❗ **Ci vuole una fotografia formato tessera.** tshē vōō·ō'le ōō'nä fōtōgräfē'ä förmä'tō te'serä.
>
> You'll need a passport photo.

Where can I get a passport photo made?	**Dove posso fare delle fotografie formato tessera?** dō've po'sō fä're de'le fōtōgräfē'e förmä'tō te'serä?
When is the half-day pass valid?	**Da che ora è valido lo ski-pass per mezza giornata?** dä ke ō'rä e vä'lēdō lō skē'päs per me'tsä jörnä'tä?
When is the last downhill run?	**A che ora c'è l'ultima discesa a valle?** ä ke ō'rä tshe lōōl'tēmä dēshe'sä ä vä'le?

182

When do the lifts *start/stop* running?	**Da/Fino a che ora funziona la sciovia?** dä/fē'nō ä ke ō'rä fōōntsyō'nä lä shēōvē'ä?
Has the cross-country skiing track been laid down?	**La pista di fondo è tracciata?** lä pē'stä dē fōn'dō e trätshä'tä?

Skiing

avalanche warning	**il pericolo di valanghe** ēl perē'kōlō dē välän'ge
binding	**l'attacco** lätä'kō
chair lift	**la seggiovia** lä sejōvē'ä
cross-country skiing	**lo sci di fondo** lō shē dē fōn'dō
cross-country track	**la pista di fondo** lä pē'stä dē fōn'dō
downhill run	**la discesa** lä dēshe'sä
ice	**il ghiaccio** ēl gyä'tshō
– skating	**pattinare** pätēnä're
icy	**ghiacciato** gyätshä'tō
lift pass	**lo ski-pass** lō skē'päs
children's –	**lo ski-pass per bambini** lō skē'päs per bämbē'nē
half-day –	**lo ski-pass per mezza giornata** lō skē'päs per me'tsä jōrnä'tä
week –	**lo ski-pass settimanale** lō skē'päs setēmänä'le
piste	**la pista** lä pō'ctä
black –	**la pista nera** lä pē'stä ne'rä
blue –	**la pista blu** lä pē'stä blōō
red –	**la pista rossa** lä pē'stä rō'ssä

183

poma lift	**la sciovia** lä shēōvē'ä
ski lift	**la sciovia** lä shēōvē'ä
ski poles	**i bastoncini** ē bästōntshē'nē
ski wax	**la sciolina** lä shēōlē'nä
skiing	**lo sci** lō shē
– goggles	**gli occhiali da sci** lyē ōkyä'lē dä shē
– instructor	**il maestro di sci** ēl mä-es'trō dē shē
– lessons	**il corso di sci** ēl kōr'sō dē shē
snow	**la neve** lä ne've
to go tobogganing	**andare in slitta** ändä're ēn slē'tä
toboggan course	**la pista per slitte** lä pē'stä per slē'te
tow lift	**lo ski-lift** lō skē'lēft

MORE SPORTS AND GAMES

Do you have any *playing cards/ board games*?	**Ha *delle carte da gioco/dei giochi di società*?** ä de'le kär'te dä jō'kō/de'ē jō'kē dē sōtshetä'?
What sports do you participate in?	**Che sport pratica Lei?** ke spōrt prä'tēkä le'ē?
Do you play chess?	**Gioca a scacchi?** jō'kä ä skä'kē?
I'd like to take a … course.	**Vorrei fare un corso di …** vōre'ē fä're ōōn kōr'sō dē …
May I join in?	**Posso giocare anch'io?** pō'sō jōkä're änke'ō?

We'd like to rent a *tennis/squash* court for *an hour/half an hour*. | **Vorremmo avere un campo da *tennis/squash* per *un'ora/mezz'ora*.** vōre'mō äve're ōōn käm'pō dä te'nēs/skōō-ōsh' per ōōnō'rä/metsō'rä.

I'd like to rent … | **Vorrei noleggiare …** vōre'ē nōlejä're …

Sports and Games

athletic	**sportivo** spōrtē'vō
badminton	**il badminton** ēl bed'mēntōn
bait	**l'esca** le'skä
ball	**la palla** lä pä'lä
basketball	**la pallacanestro** lä päläkänes'trō
beginner *(female)*	**la principiante** lä prēntshēpyän'te
beginner *(male)*	**il principiante** ēl prēntshēpyän'te
bicycle	**la bicicletta** lä bētshēkle'tä
bike hike	**il giro in bicicletta** ēl jē'rō ēn bētshēkle'tä
bowling	**il bowling** ēl bōō'lēng
canoe	**la canoa** lä känō'ä
card game	**la partita a carte** lä pärtē'tä ä kär'te
changing rooms	**gli spogliatoi** lyē spōlyätoi'
coach	**l'allenatore** lälenätō're
competition	**la gara** lä gä'rä
course	**il corso** ēl kōr'sō
to cycle, to go cycling	**andare in bicicletta** ändä're ēn bētshēkle'tä
finishing line	**il traguardo** ēl trägōō-är'dō
first half *(of a game)*	**il primo tempo** ēl prē'mō tem'pō

to go fishing	**andare a pesca** ändä're ä pes'kä
fishing license	**la licenza di pesca**
	lä lētshen'tsä dē pe'skä
fishing rod	**la canna da pesca** lä kä'nä dä pe'skä
game	**la partita** lä pärte'tä
goal	**il goal** ēl gōl
– keeper	**il portiere** ēl pōrtye're
golf	**il golf** ēl gōlf
– club	**la mazza da golf** lä mä'tsä dä gōlf
– course	**il campo da golf** ēl käm'pō dä gōlf
gymnastics	**la ginnastica** lä jēnä'stēkä
handball	**la palla a mano** lä pä'lä ä mä'nō
hang-gliding	**lo sport del deltaplano**
	lō spōrt del deltäplä'nō
horse	**il cavallo** ēl kävä'lō
jazz dancing	**la danza jazz** lä dän'tsä jets
to jog	**fare jogging** fä're jō'gēng
kayak	**il kayak** ēl käyäk'
to lose	**perdere** per'dere
mini-golf course	**la pista di minigolf**
	lä pē'stä dē mēnēgōlf'
paragliding	**il parapendio** ēl päräpendē'ō
to play	**giocare** jōkä're
to go rafting	**il rafting** ēl räf'tēn
referee	**l'arbitro** lär'bētrō
regatta	**la regata** lä regä'tä
to ride a horse	**cavalcare** kävälkä're
second half	**il secondo tempo** ēl sekōn'dō tem'pō
(of a game)	

skydiving	**il paracadutismo** ēl päräkädōōtēz'mō
soccer	**il calcio** ēl käl'tshō
– field	**il campo di calcio** ēl käm'pō dē käl'tshō
– game	**la partita di calcio** lä pärtē'tä dē käl'tshō
sports	**lo sport** lō spōrt
– studio	**la palestra** lä päles'trä
– field	**il campo sportivo** ēl käm'pō spōrtē'vō
squash	**lo squash** lō skōō-ōsh'
– ball	**la palla da squash** lä pä'lä dä skōō-ōsh'
– court	**il campo da squash** ēl käm'pō dä skōō-ōsh'
– raquet	**la racchetta da squash** lä räke'tä dä skōō-ōsh'
start	**la partenza** lä pärten'tsä
table tennis	**il ping-pong** ēl pēng-pōng'
team	**la squadra** lä skōō-ä'drä
tennis	**il tennis** ēl te'nēs
– ball	**la palla da tennis** lä pä'lä dä te'nēs
– court	**il campo da tennis** ēl käm'pō dä te'nēs
– racket	**la racchetta da tennis** lä räke'tä dä te'nēs
victory	**la vittoria** lä vētōr'yä
volleyball	**la pallavolo** lä pälävō'lō
to win	**vincere** vēn'tshere

7

CULTURE AND FESTIVALS

At the Box Office

centro tshen'trō	middle
destra des'trä	right
Entrata enträ'tä	entrance
eusaurito esoure'tō	sold out
Fila fē'lä	row
Galleria gälerē'ä	level
Palco päl'kō	box
Platea pläte'ä	orchestra
Posto pō'stō	seat
sinistra sēnēs'trä	left
Uscita di sicurezza ōōshē'tä dē sēkōōre'tsä	emergency exit

INFO In the summer, there are theatrical performances and concerts in ancient amphitheaters; for example, in Taormina or Verona. Almost every village or town holds a **sagra** (folk festival) in which food typical of the region is celebrated; for example in the **sagra del gambero** sä'grä del gäm'berō (festival of prawns). The event often starts off with a parade and ends with fireworks (**fuochi d'artificio** fōō·ō'kē därtēfē'tshō).

In many towns there are also traditional festivals, during which actors wear historical costumes; for example in the **calcio storico fiorentino** käl'tshō stō'rēkō fyōrente'no (medieval soccer game) in Florence, or in the **corsa dei ceri** kōr'sä de'ē tshe'rē (a race with giant candles) in Gubbio.

Do you have a schedule of events?	**Ha un programma delle manifestazioni?** ä ōōn prōgrä′mä de′le mänēfestätsyō′nē?
Where can I get tickets?	**Dove si comprano i biglietti?** dō′ve sē kōm′pränō ē bēlye′tē?
When does the *performance/concert* start?	**A che ora inizia *lo spettacolo/il concerto*?** ä ke ō′rä ēnē′tsyä *lō spetä′kōlō/ēl kōntsher′tō*?
When is general admission?	**Da che ora si può entrare?** dä ke ō′rä sē pōō-ō′ enträ′re?
Are the seats numbered?	**I posti sono numerati?** ē pō′stē sō′nō nōōmerä′tē?
Can I reserve tickets?	**Si possono riservare dei biglietti?** sē pō′sōnō rēservä′re de′ē bēlye′tē?
Do you still have tickets for *today/tomorrow*?	**Ci sono ancora dei biglietti per *oggi/domani*?** tshē sō′nō änkō′rä de′ē bēlye′tē per *ō′jē/dōmä′nē*?
How much is a ticket?	**Quanto costa il biglietto?** kōō·än′tō kō′stä ēl bēlye′tō?
Is there a discount for …	**C'è una riduzione per …** tshe ōō′nä rēdōōtsyō′ne per …
children?	**bambini?** bämbē′nē?
senior citizens?	**gli anziani?** lyē äntsyä′nē?
students?	**gli studenti?** lyē stōōden′tē?

7

189

I'd like *one ticket/two tickets* for …	**Un biglietto/Due biglietti per …, per favore.** ōōn bēlye'tō/dōō'e bēlye'tē per …, per fävō're.	

today.	**oggi** ō'jē
this evening.	**stasera** stäse'rä
the matinee.	**la matinée** lä mätēne'
tomorrow.	**domani** dōmä'nē
the day after tomorrow.	**dopodomani** dōpodōmä'nē

When is the performance over?	**A che ora finisce lo spettacolo?** ä ke ō'rä fēnē'she lō spetä'kōlō?
I'd like to rent an opera glass.	**Vorrei prendere in prestito un binocolo da teatro.** vōre'ē pren'dere ēn pre'stētō ōōn bēnō'kōlō dä te-ä'trō.

Culture and Festivals

act	**l'atto** lä'tō
actor	**l'attore** *m* lätō're
actress	**l'attrice** *f* lätrē'tshe
advance booking	**la prevendita** lä preven'dētä
ballet	**il balletto** ēl bäle'tō
beginning	**l'inizio** lēnē'tsyō
box office	**la cassa** lä kä'sä
cabaret	**il cabaret** ēl käbäre'
chamber music	**la musica da camera** lä mōōsēkä dä kä'merä
choir	**il coro** ēl kō'rō

190

circus	**il circo** ēl tshēr'kō	
cloakroom	**il guardaroba** ēl gōō-ärdärō'bä	
comedy	**la commedia** lä kōme'dyä	
composer *(female)*	**la compositrice** lä kōmpōsētrē'tshe	
composer *(male)*	**il compositore** ēl kōmpōsētō're	
concert	**il concerto** ēl kōntsher'tō	
– hall	**la sala da concerti** lä sä'lä dä kōntsher'tē	
conductor	**il direttore d'orchestra** ēl dēretō're dōrkes'trä	**7**
dancer *(male)*	**il ballerino** ēl bälerē'nō	
dancer *(female)*	**la ballerina** lä bälerē'nä	
director *(male)*	**il regista** ēl rejē'stä	
director *(female)*	**la regista** lä rejē'sta	
discount	**la riduzione** lä rēdōōtsyō'ne	
dubbed	**doppiato** dōpyä'tō	
end	**la fine** lä fē'ne	
folklore evening	**la serata folkloristica** lä serä'tä fōlklōrē'stēkä	
grand piano	**il pianoforte a coda** ēl pyänōfōr'te ä kō'dä	
intermission	**l'intervallo** lēntervä'lō	
leading role	**il ruolo principale** ēl rōō-ō'lō prēntshēpä'le	
movie	**il film** ēl fēlm	
– theater	**il cinema** ēl tshē'nemä	
music	**la musica** lä mōō'zēkä	
musical *(play)*	**il musical** ēl myōō'zēkōl	
open-air theater	**il teatro all'aperto** ēl te-ä'trō äläper'tō	

opera	**l'opera** lō'perä
operetta	**l'operetta** lōpere'tä
orchestra	**l'orchestra** lōrkes'trä
to perform	**recitare** retshētä're
performance	**lo spettacolo** lō spetä'kōlō
play	**l'opera teatrale** lō'perä te-äträ'le
to play *(music)*	**suonare** sōō-ōnä're
premiere	**la prima** lä prē'mä
program	**il programma** ēl prōgrä'mä
seat	**il posto** ēl pō'stō
singer *(male)*	**il cantante** ēl käntän'te
singer *(female)*	**la cantante** lä käntän'te
stage	**il palcoscenico** ēl pälkōshe'nēkō
subtitled	**con i sottotitoli** kōn ē sōtōtē'tōlē
theater	**il teatro** ēl te-ä'trō
ticket	**il biglietto (d'ingresso)** ēl bēlye'tō (dēngre'sō)
variety show	**il varietà** ēl väryetä'
vocal recital	**la serata liederistica** lä serä'tä lēdere'stēkä

GOING OUT IN THE EVENING

Is there a nice bar around here?	**C'è un locale simpatico da queste parti?** tshe ōōn lōkä'le sēmpä'tēkō dä kōō-e'ste pär'tē?
Where can you go dancing around here?	**Dove si può andare a ballare da queste parti?** dō've sē pōō-ō' ändä're ä bälä're dä kōō-e'ste pär'tē?

192

May I sit here?	**È libero qui?** e lē'berō kōō-ē'?	
Can you get something to eat here?	**Si può anche mangiare qualcosa qui?** sē pōō-ō' än'ke mänjä're kōō-älkō'sä kōō-ē'?	
Do you have a drinks menu?	**Ha una carta delle bevande?** ä ōō'nä kär'tä de'le bevän'de?	

> **!** **Nel biglietto d'ingresso è inclusa una consumazione.** nel bēlye'tō dēngre'sō e ēnklōō'zä ōō'nä kōnzōōmätsyō'ne. | A drink is included in the price of the ticket. **7**

I'd like a *beer/glass of wine*, please.	*Una birra/Un bicchiere di vino*, **per favore.** ōō'nä bē'rä/ōōn bēkye're dē vē'nō, per fävō're.	
The same again, please.	**Un altro, per favore.** ōōn äl'trō, per fävō're.	
What would you like to drink?	*Che cosa Le/ti andrebbe di bere?* ke kō'sä *le/tē* ändre'be dē be're?	
May *I* buy *you* something to drink?	*Le/Ti* **posso offrire qualcosa da bere?** *le/tē* pō'sō ōfrē're kōō-älkō'sä dä be're?	

➡ *see also: Food and Drink (p. 107)*

Would you like to dance?	*Vuole/Vuoi* **ballare?** *vōō-ōle/vōō-ōi' bälä'*ıe?	
You dance very well.	*Balla/Balli* **molto bene.** *bä'lä/bä'lē* mōl'tō be'ne.	

193

Going out in the Evening

bar *(counter)*	**il bar** ēl bär
bistro	**il locale** ēl lōkä'le
casino	**il casinò** ēl käsēnō'
dance	**il ballo** ēl bä'lō
to dance	**ballare** bälä're
disco	**la discoteca** lä dēskōte'kä
to drink	**bere** be're
evening dress	**l'abito da sera** lä'bētō dä se'rä

Post Office and Bank

POST, TELEGRAMS, TELEPHONE

Letters and Parcels

Where is the nearest mailbox?	**Dov'è la cassetta postale più vicina?** dōve' lä käse'tä pōstä'le pyōō vētshē'nä
Where is the nearest post office?	**Dov'è l'ufficio postale più vicino?** dōve' lōōfē'tshō pōstä'le pyōō vētshē'nō?
How much does a *letter/postcard* to the United States cost?	**Quanto costa spedire una *lettera/cartolina* per l'America?** kōō·än'tō kō'stä spedē're ōō'nä *le'terä/kärtōlē'nä* per läme'rēkä?
Five ... stamps, please.	**Cinque francobolli da ... , per favore.** tshēn'kōō·e fränkōbō'lē dä ..., per fävō're.
I'd like to mail this *letter/package* ..., please.	**Vorrei spedire *questa lettera/questo pacchetto* ...** vōre'ē spedē're *kōō·e'stä le'terä/kōō·e'stō* päke'tō ...
by registered mail	**per raccomandata.** per räkōmändä'tä.
by airmail	**per via aerea.** per vē'ä ä·e're·ä.
by express mail	**per espresso.** per espre'sō.
I'd like to send a package.	**Vorrei spedire un pacco.** vōre'ē spedē're ōōn pä'kō.
Where is the general-delivery counter?	**Dov'è lo sportello del fermo posta?** dōve' lō spōrte'lō del fer'mō pō'stä?

196

| Is there any mail for me? | **C'è posta per me?** tshe pō'stä per me? |

The Line Home

Can I send a telegram from here?	**Vorrei mandare un telegramma.** **Posso farlo qui?** vōre'ē mändä're ōōn telegrä'mä. pô'sō tär'lō kōō-ē'?
Please give me a form for a telegram.	**Un modulo per telegrammi, per favore.** ōōn mō'dōōlō per telegrä'mē, per fävō're.
Where can I make a phone call?	**Dov'è che si può telefonare qui?** dōve' ke sē pōō-ô' telefōnä're kōō-ē'?

INFO In Italy you will find telephones at post offices, bars, and tobacconist's. These will be marked by a yellow sign with a phone receiver. Most telephones use either cards or coins; recently phones have been installed that only use telephone cards. You can get a telephone card (**carta telefonica** kär'tä telefō'nēkä) at the post office and tobacconist's. Before you can use it, you must break off (**strappare** sträpä're) one corner of the card.

8

| Could you tell me where I might find a phone booth? | **Mi saprebbe dire per favore dov'è una cabina telefonica?** mē säpre'be dē're per fävō're dōve' ōō'nä käbē'nä telefō'nēkä? |

! **Vada alla cabina ...** vä'dä ä'lä käbē'nä ...

Go into booth ...

197

Where can I get a telephone card?	**Dove posso comprare una carta telefonica?** dō've pō'sō kōmprä're ōō'nä kär'tä telefō'nēkä?
Could you give me some change for this bill?	**Mi potrebbe cambiare questa banconota?** mē pōtre'be kämbyä're kōō·e'stä bänkōnō'tä?
What's the area code for …?	**Qual è il prefisso di …?** kōō·äl' e ēl prefē'sō dē …?

INFO In order to phone someone in the United States, first dial 001 (international code + code for the US and Canada), then the area code (without any further prefix), and then the telephone number.

! **La linea è *occupata/disturbata*.** • lä lē'ne·ä e ōkōōpä'tä/dēstōōrbä'tä.	The line is *busy/out of order*.
! **Non risponde nessuno.** • nōn rēspōn'de nesōō'nō.	There's no answer.
! **Provi ancora una volta.** • prō've änkō'rä ōō'nä vōl'tä.	You'll have to try again.

When do evening rates apply?	**Da che ora è valida la tariffa notturna?** dä ke ō'rä e vä'lēdä lä tärē'fä nōtōōr'nä?
I'd like to place a call to the United States.	**Vorrei fare una telefonata in America.** vōre'ē fä're ōō'nä telefōnä'tä ēn äme'rēkä.

addressee	**il destinatario**	ēl destēnätär'yō
area code	**il prefisso**	ēl prefē'sō
busy	**occupato**	ōkōōpä'tō
by airmail	**via aerea**	vē'ä ä·e're·ä
charge	**la tariffa**	lä tärē'fä
COD	**il contrassegno**	ēl kōnträseṅ'yō
collect call	**la telefonata a carico del ricevente**	
	lä telefōnä'tä ä kä'rēkō del rētsheven'te	
to connect *(a call)*	**passare**	päsä're
counter	**lo sportello**	lō spōrte'lō
envelope	**la busta**	lä bōō'stä
express letter	**l'espresso**	lespre'sō
fax	**il telefax**	ēl te'lefäks
international call	**la telefonata internazionale**	
	lä telefōnä'tä ēnternätsyōnä'le	
letter	**la lettera**	lä le'terä
mailbox	**la cassetta delle lettere**	
	lä käse'tä de'le le'tere	
package	**il pacco**	ēl pä'kō
– info form	**il bollettino di spedizione dei pacchi postali**	
	ēl bōletē'nō dē spedētsyō'ne de'ē pä'kē pōstä'lē	
parcel	**il pacchetto**	ēl päke'tō
pay phone	**il telefono a monete**	ēl tele'fōnō ä mone'te
phone that operates with a phone card	**il telefono a schede**	ēl tele'fōnō ä ske'de

8

199

post office	**la posta** lä pō'stä
postcard	**la cartolina (illustrata)**
	lä kärtōlē'nä (ēlōōsträ'tä)
to send	**spedire** spedē're
stamp	**il francobollo** ēl fränkōbō'lō
– vending machine	**il distributore automatico di francobolli** ēl dēstrēbōōtō're outōmä'tēkō dē fränkōbō'lē
telegram	**il telegramma** ēl telegrä'mä
telephone	**il telefono** ēl tele'fōnō
– booth	**la cabina telefonica** lä käbē'nä telefō'nēkä
– card	**la carta telefonica** lä kär'tä telefō'nēkä
– conversation	**la telefonata** lä telefōnä'tä
– directory	**l'elenco telefonico** lelen'kō telefō'nēkō
– number	**il numero di telefono** ēl nōō'merō dē telefō'nō
to make a telephone call	**telefonare** telefōnä're
ZIP code	**il codice di avviamento postale** ēl kō'dētshe dē ävyämen'tō pōstä'le

MONEY MATTERS

Can you tell me where I can find a bank around here?	**Scusi, c'è una banca qui vicino?** skōō'zē, tshe ōō'nä bän'kä kōō-e' vētshē'nō?
Where can I exchange foreign currency?	**Dove posso cambiare dei soldi?** dō've pô'sō kämbyä're de'ē sōl'dē?
What's the commission charge?	**A quanto ammontano le spese bancarie?** ä kōō·än'tō ämōn'tänō le spe'se bänkär'ye?
What time does the bank close?	**Fino a che ora è aperta la banca?** fē'nō ä ke ō'rä e äper'tä lä bän'kä?

8

INFO Banks are open from Monday to Friday in the morning until 1 p.m., and then again in the afternoon for only one hour. You can also exchange money at an **agenzia di cambio** äjen'tsyä dē käm'byō. It has longer opening hours than a bank, but it has also a less advantageous exchange rate.

I'd like to change … dollars into euros.	**Vorrei cambiare … dollari in euro.** vōre'ē kämbyä're … dōl'äre ēn e'ōōrō.
Someone is wiring me money. Has it arrived yet?	**Mi sono fatto mandare un vaglia telegrafico. È già arrivato?** mē sō'nō fä'tō mändä're ōōn vä'lyä telegrä'fēkō. e jä ärēvä'tō?

201

Can I use my credit card to get cash?	**Posso avere del denaro in contanti con la mia carta di credito?** pö'sö äve're del denä'rö ēn kôntän'tē kôn lä mē'ä kär'tä dē kre'dētö?

I'd like to cash a traveler's check.	**Vorrei riscuotere un traveller's cheque.** vôre'ē rēskoō-öte're oōn trä'velers·shek.

! *Il Suo passaporto/La Sua carta d'identità, per favore.*
* ēl soō'ö päsäpôr'to/lä soō'ä kär'tä dēdentētä', per fävö're.

May I see your *passport/ID*, please?

! **Firmi qui, per favore.**
* fēr'mē koō-ē', per fävö're.

Would you sign here, please?

! **Per ritirare il denaro si accomodi alla cassa.** per rētērä're ēl denä'rö sē äkö'mödē ä'lä kä'sä.

You can pick up the money at the cashier.

? **Che tagli preferisce?**
* ke tä'lyē frefere'she?

How would you like the money?

In small bills, please.	**Banconote di piccolo taglio, per favore.** bänkönö'te dē pē'kölö tä'lyö, per fävö're.

Please give me some change, too.	**Mi dia anche un po' di spiccioli, per favore.** mē dē'ä än'ke oōn pö dē spē'tshölē, per fävö're.

ATM	**la cassa automatica prelievi**
	lä kä'sä outōmä''tēkä prelye've
bank	**la banca** lä bän'kä
– account	**il conto in banca**
	ēl kōn'tō ēn bän'kä
– code	**il codice di avviamento bancario**
	ēl kodetshe bänkärēō bänkär'yō
– transfer	**il bonifico (bancario)**
	ēl bōnēfēkō (bänkär'yō)
bill	**la banconota** lä bänkönō'tä
card number	**il numero della carta assegni**
	ēl nōō'merō de'lä kär'tä äse'nyē
cash	**il denaro in contanti**
	ēl denä'rō ēn köntän'tē
cashier	**la cassa** lä kä'sä
change	**gli spiccioli** lyē spē'tshōle
check	**l'assegno** läse'nyō
check card	**la carta assegni** lä kär'tä äse'nyē
PIN	**il numero segreto**
	ēl nōō'mero segre'tō
commission	**la tariffa** lä tärē'fä
counter	**lo sportello** lō spörte'lō
credit card	**la carta di credito** lä kär'tä dē kredē'tō
currency exchange	**l'agenzia di cambio**
	läjen'tsyä dē käm'byō
dollar	**il dollaro** ēl dō'lärō
to exchange	**cambiare** kämbyä're
exchange rate	**il cambio** ēl käm'byō

money	**il denaro, i soldi** ēl denä'rō, ē sōl'dē
savings account	**il libretto di risparmio**
	ēl lēbre'tō dē rēspär'myō
savings bank	**la cassa di risparmio**
	lä kä'sä dē rēspär'myō
signature	**la firma** lä fēr'mä
total amount	**l'importo** lēmpōr'tō
traveler's check	**il traveller's cheque** ēl tre'velers·shek
to withdraw	**prelevare** prelevä're

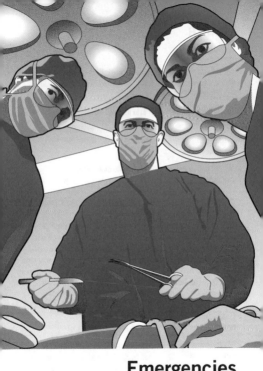

Emergencies

HEALTH

Information

Could you recommend a general practitioner?	**Mi può consigliare un medico generico?** mē pōō·ō kōnsēlyä′re ōon me′dēkō jene′rēkō?
Does *he/she* speak English?	**Parla inglese?** pär′lä ēn·gle′se?
What are *his/her* office hours?	**Quando riceve?** kōō·än′dō rētshe′ve?
Where is *his/her* practice?	**Dov'è il suo ambulatorio?** dōve′ ēl sōō′ō ämbōōlätor′yō?

INFO If there is an accident, you must contact the **pronto soccorso** prōn′tō sōkōr′sō (first aid) of the nearest hospital, and they will pick up the injured person in an ambulance. If someone is seriously ill, get in touch with the **guardia medica** gōō·är′dyä me′dēkä, the local doctor on call for emergencies, who will visit the patient at home. If you don't know what to do, the **carabinieri** käräbēnye′rē (police) will help you; they can be reached at telephone number 113 anywhere in Italy.

Can *he/she* make house calls?	**Fa visite a domicilio?** fä vēze′tē ä dōmētshē′lyō?
My *husband/wife* is sick.	**Mio marito/Mia moglie sta male.** mē′ō märē′tō/mē′ä mō′lye stä mä′le.

206

Please call *an ambulance*/*the emergency doctor*!	**Chiami *un'ambulanza*/*la guardia medica*!** kyä'me ōōnämbōōlän'tsä/lä gōō·är'dyä me'dēkä!
Where are you taking *him*/*her*?	**Dove *lo*/*la* portate?** dō've lō/lä pōrtä'te?
I'd like to come with you.	**Vorrei venire anch'io.** vōre'ē venē're änke'ō.
Where's the nearest (24-hour) pharmacy?	**Dov'è la farmacia (con servizio notturno) più vicina?** dōve' lä färmätshē'ä (kōn serve'tsyō nōtōōr'nō) pyōō vētshē'nä?

Drugstore

| Do you have anything for …? | **Ha qualcosa contro …?** ä kōō·älkō'sä kōn'trō …? |

> *Diseases, Doctor, Hospital (p. 219)*

| *How*/*When* should I take it? | ***Come*/*Quando* la devo prendere?** kō'me/kōō·än'dō lä de'vō pren'dere? |
| I need this medicine. | **Mi serve questa medicina.** mē ser've kōō·e'stä medētshē'nä. |

| ! | **Per questa medicina ci vuole la ricetta.** por kōō·e'stä medētshē'nä tshē vōō·ō'le lä rētshe'tä. | You need a prescription for this medicine. |
| ! | **Al momento non l'abbiamo.** äl mōmen'tō nōn läbyä'mō. | I'm sorry, but we don't have that here. |

9

207

!	**Dobbiamo ordinarlo.**	We'll have to order it.
●	dōbyä′mō ōrdēnär′lō.	

When can I pick it up?	**Quando posso averla?**
	kōō·än′dō pō′sō äver′lä?

Patient Package Insert

a digiuno, a stomaco vuoto	on an empty stomach
ä dejōō′nō, ä stō′mäkō vōō-ō′tō	
dopo i pasti dō′pō ē pä′stē	after meals
effetti collaterali efē′tē kōläterä′lē	side effects
far sciogliere in bocca	allow to dissolve on
fär shō′lyere ēn bō′kä	the tongue
per uso esterno per ōō′zō ester′nō	external
per uso interno per ōō′zō ēnter′nō	internal
per via rettale per vē′ä retä′le	rectally
prima dei pasti prē′mä de′ē pä′stē	before meals
secondo le indicazioni del medico	according to the
sekōn′dō le ēndēkätsyō′nē del me′dēkō	doctor's instructions
senza masticare sen′tsä mästēkä′re	swallow whole
tre volte al giorno tre vōl′te äl jōr′nō	three times a day

Drugstore

alcohol	**l'alcool (denaturato)** *m*
	läl′kō-ōl (denätōōrä′tō)
antibiotic	**l'antibiotico** läntēbē-ō′tēkō
antiseptic ointment	**la pomata per le ferite**
	lä pōmä′tä per le ferē′te

Band-Aid®	**il cerotto** ēl tshērō'tō
birth-control pill	**la pillola anticoncezionale** lä pēˈlōlä äntēkōntshetsyōnäˈle
charcoal tablets	**le compresse al carbone vegetale** le kōmpreˈse äl kärbōˈne vejetäˈle
circulatory stimulant	**un farmaco contro i disturbi circolatori** ōōn färˈmäko kōnˈtrō ē dēstōōrˈbē tshērkōlätōˈre
condoms	**i profilattici, i preservativi** ē prōfēläˈtētshē, ē preservätēˈvē
cotton	**il cotone idrofilo** ēl kōtōˈne ēdrōˈfēlō
cough syrup	**lo sciroppo per la tosse** lō shērōˈpō per lä tōˈse
disinfectant	**il disinfettante** ēl dēsēnfetänˈte
drops	**le gocce** le gōˈtshe
elastic bandage	**la benda elastica** lä benˈdä eläˈstēkä
fever	**la febbre** lä feˈbre
medicine to reduce –	**l'antipiretico** läntēpēreˈtēkō
first-aid kit	**le bende** le benˈde
gauze bandage	**la garza** lä gärˈtsä
homeopathic	**omeopatico** ōme-ōpäˈtēkō
iodine	**lo iodio** lō yōˈdyō
laxative	**il lassativo** ēl läsätēˈvō
night duty	**il servizio notturno** ēl servēˈtsyō nōtōōrˈnō
ointment	**la pomata** lä pōmäˈtä
– for mosquito bites	**la pomata contro le punture di zanzare** lä pōmäˈtä kōnˈtrō le pōōntōōˈre dē dzändzäˈre

9

209

– for sun allergy	**la pomata contro l'eritema solare**
	lä pōmä'tä kōn'trō lerēte'mä sōlä're
painkiller	**l'analgesico** lä'nälje'sēkō
pharmacy	**la farmacia** lä färmätshē'ä
powder	**la polverina** lä pōlverē'nä
prescription	**la ricetta** lä rētshe'tä
sanitary napkins	**gli assorbenti igienici**
	lyē äsōrben'tē ēj·e'nētshē
sleeping pills	**il sonnifero** ēl sōne'ferō
something for …	**qualcosa contro …** kōō·älkō'sä kōn'trō …
suppository	**la supposta** lä sōōpō'stä
tablet	**la compressa** lä kōmpre'sä
talcum powder	**il borotalco** ēl bōrōtäl'kō
tampons	**i tamponi** ē tämpō'nē
thermometer	**il termometro** ēl termō'metrō
tranquilizer	**il calmante** ēl kälmän'te

➡ *see also:* Diseases, Doctor, Hospital (S. 219)

At the Doctor's

| I have a (bad) cold. | **Ho un (forte) raffreddore.** |
| | ō ōōn (fōr'te) räfredō're. |

| I have *diarrhea/* *a (high) fever*. | **Ho la diarrea/febbre (alta).** |
| | ō lä dyäre'ä/fe'bre (äl'tä). |

| I don't feel well. | **Non mi sento bene.** nōn mē sen'tō be'ne. |

| I feel nauseous. | **Ho la nausea.** ō lä näōō'seä. |

| I'm dizzy. | **Mi gira la testa.** mē jē'rä lä te'stä. |

INFO Address doctors only by their title of **dottore**
dōtōʹre, or **dotoressa** dōtōreʹsä if the doctor is a woman.

My … hurts/hurt.	**Mi** *fa*/*fanno* **male** … mē *fä*/*fäʹnō* mäʹle …

➡ *Parts of the Body and Organs (p. 217)*

I have pains here.	**Ho dei dolori qui.** ō deʹē dōlōʹrē kōō-ēʹ.
I've been vomiting (a lot).	**Ho vomitato (più volte).** ō vōmētäʹtō (pyōō vōlʹte).
My stomach is upset.	**Ho fatto indigestione.** ō fäʹtō ēndējestyōʹne.
I fainted.	**Sono** ♂**svenuto**/♀**svenuta.** sōʹnō ♂ zvenōōʹtō/♀ zvenōōʹtä.
I can't move …	**Non posso muovere** … nōn pōʹsō mōō-ōʹvere …

➡ *Parts of the Body and Organs (p. 217)*

I've hurt myself.	**Mi sono** ♂**ferito**/♀**ferita.** mē sōʹnō ♂ ferēʹtō/♀ ferēʹtä.
I had a fall.	**Sono** ♂**caduto**/♀**caduta.** sōʹnō ♂ kädōōʹtō/♀ kädōōʹtä.
I've been *stung*/*bitten* by …	**Mi ha** *punto*/*morso* … mē ä *pōōnʹtō*/*mōrʹsō* …

9

211

What you should tell the doctor

I have (not) been vaccinated against …	**(Non) sono ♂ vaccinato/♀ vaccinata contro …** (nōn) sō'nō ♂ vätshēnä'tō/♀ vätshēnä'tä kōn'trō …
I'm allergic to penicillin.	**Sono ♂ allergico/♀ allergica alla penicillina.** sō'nō ♂ äler'jēkō/♀ äler'jēkä ä'lä penētshēlē'nä.
I have *high*/*low* blood pressure.	**Ho la pressione *alta*/*bassa*.** ō lä presyō'ne *äl'tä*/*bä'sä*.
I have a pacemaker.	**Ho il pace-maker.** ō ēl pēēs'mekä.
I'm … months pregnant.	**Sono al … mese di gravidanza.** sō'nō äl … me'se dē grävēdän'tsä.
I'm diabetic.	**Sono ♂ diabetico/♀ diabetica.** sō'nō ♂ dē-äbe'tēkō/♀ dē-äbe'tēkä.
I'm HIV-positive.	**Sono ♂ sieropositivo/♀ sieropositiva.** sō'nō ♂ syerōpōsētē'vō ♀ syerōpōsētē'vä.
I take this medicine regularly.	**Prendo regolarmente queste medicine.** pren'dō regōlärmen'te kōō·e'ste medētshē'ne.

What the doctor says

Che disturbi ha? ke dēstŏŏr′bē ä?	What are your symptoms?
Dov'è che le fa male? dōve′ ke le fä mä′le?	Where does it hurt?
Le da fastidio? le da fästlē′dyō?	Does that hurt?
Apra la bocca. ä′prä lä bō′kä.	Open your mouth, please.
Mi faccia vedere la lingua. mē fä′tshä vede′re lä lēn′gōō·ä.	Show me your tongue, please.
Tossisca. tōsē′skä.	Cough.
Si spogli, per favore. sē spō′lyē, per fävō′re.	Would you get undressed, please.
Scopra il braccio, per favore. skō′prä ēl brä′tshō, per fävō′re.	Would you roll up your sleeve, please.
Respiri profondamente. Trattenga il respiro. respē′rē prōfōndämen′te. träten′gä ēl respē′rō.	Breathe deeply. Now hold your breath.
Da quanto tempo ha questi disturbi? dä kōō·än′tō tem′pō ä kōō·e′stē dēstŏŏr′bē?	How long have you felt this way?
È ♂ vaccinato/♀ vaccinata contro …? e ♂ vätshēnä′tō/♀ vätshēnä′tä kōn′trō …?	Have you been vaccinated against …?

9

213

Ha un libretto delle vaccinazioni? ä ōōn lēbre'tō de'le vätshēnatsyō'nē?	Do you have a vaccination record?
Deve fare una radiografia. de've fä're ōō'nä rädyōgräfē'ä.	We need to take some X-rays.
Si è ♂rotto/♀rotta/♂slogato/♀slogata ... sē e ♂rō'tō/♀rō'tä/♂zlōgä'tō/♀zlōgä'tä ...	Your ... is *broken/ sprained.*
Deve fare l'analisi *del sangue/delle urine.* de've fä're länäl'ēzē *del sän'gōō-e/de'le ōōrē'ne.*	We need to take a *blood/urine* sample.
Deve operarsi. de've ōperär'sē.	You'll have to have an operation.
Deve andare da uno specialista. de've ändä're dä ōō'nō spetshäle'stä.	I'll have to refer you to a specialist.
Non è niente di grave. nōn e nēen'te dē grä've.	It's nothing serious.
Prenda ... *pillole/gocce* ... volte al giorno. pren'dä ... *pē'lōle/gō'tshe* ... vōl'te äl jōr'nō.	Take ... *tablets/drops* ... times a day.
Torni *domani/fra* ... giorni. tōr'nē *dōmä'nē/frä* ... jōr'nē.	Come back *tomorrow/in* ... days.

214

Is it serious?	**È grave?** e grä've?
Can you give me a doctor's certificate?	**Mi può rilasciare un certificato medico?** mē pōō-ō' rēläshä're ōōn tshertēfēkä'tō me'dēkō?
Do I have to come back again?	**Devo tornare ancora?** de'vō tōrnä're änkō'rä?
What precautions should I take?	**A che cosa devo fare attenzione?** ä ke kō'sä de'vō fä're ätentzyō'ne?
I need a receipt in English for my medical insurance.	**Ho bisogno di una ricevuta (in inglese) per la mia assicurazione.** ō bēzō'nyō dē ōō'nä rētshevōō'tä ēn ēn·gle'se per lä mē'ä äsēkōōrätsyō'ne.

In the Hospital

Is there anyone here who speaks English?	**C'è qualcuno che parla inglese?** tshe kōō-älkōō'nō ke pär'lä ēn·gle'se?
I'd like to speak to a doctor.	**Vorrei parlare con un dottore.** vōre'ē pärlä're kōn ōōn dōtō're.

➡ *At the Doctor's (p. 210)*

What's the diagnosis?	**Qual è la diagnosi?** kōō·äl' e lä dē·ä'nyōze?

9

215

I'd rather have the operation in the United States.	**Preferirei farmi operare in America.** preferēre'ē fär'mē operä're ēn äme'rēkä.
I'm insured for the journey home.	**Sono ♂ assicurato/ ♀ assicurata per il viaggio di ritorno.** sō'nō ♂ äsēkōōrä'tō/ ♀ äsēkōōrä'tä per ēl vyä'jo dē rētōr'nō.
Would you please notify my family?	**Avvisi la mia famiglia, per favore.** ävē'zē lä mē'ä fämē'lyä, per fävō're.
Can I have a private room?	**Posso avere una camera singola?** pō'sō ave're ōō'nä kä'merä sēn'gōlä?
How long will I have to stay here?	**Per quanto tempo devo rimanere ancora?** per kōō·än'tō tem'pō de'vō rēmäne're änkō'rä?
When can I get out of bed?	**Quando potrò alzarmi?** kōō·än'dō pōtrò' ältsär'mē?
Could you give me something *for the pain/to get to sleep*?	**Mi dia qualcosa *contro i dolori/per dormire*, per favore.** mē dē'ä kōō·älkō'sä *kōn'trō ē dōlō'rē/per dōrmē're*, per fävō're.
I'd like to be discharged. (I'll assume full responsibility.)	**Vorrei essere ♂ dimesso/ ♀ dimessa (dietro mia responsabilità).** vōre'ē e'sere ♂ dēme'sō/ ♀ dēme'sä (dye'trō mē'ä respōnsäbēlētä').

216

Please give me a certificate stating my length of stay here.

Mi rilasci un certificato con la specificazione della durata della degenza ospedaliera, per favore. mē rēlä'shē ōōn tshertēfēkä'tō kōn lä spetshēfēkätsyō'ne de'lä dōōrä'tä de'lä dejen'tsä ōspedälye'rä, per fävō're.

Parts of the Body and Organs

abdomen	**l'addome** *m* läddō'me
ankle	**il malleolo** ēl mäle'ōlō
appendix	**l'appendice** *f* läpendē'tshe
arm	**il braccio**, *pl:* **le braccia** ēl brä'tshō, *pl:* le brä'tshä
back	**la schiena** lä skye'nä
bladder	**la vescica** lä veshē'kä
blood	**il sangue** ēl sän'gōō·e
bone	**l'osso** lō'sō
brain	**il cervello** ēl tsherve'lō
bust	**il busto** ēl bōō'stō
calf	**il polpaccio** ēl polpä'tshō
cheek	**la guancia** lä gōō·än'tshä
chest	**il petto** ēl pe'tō
collarbone	**la clavicola** lä klävē'kōlä
disk	**il disco intervertebrale** ēl dō'skō ēntervertebrä'le
ear	**l'orecchio** lōre'kyō
–drum	**la membrana del timpano** lä membrä'nä del tēm'pänō
eye	**l'occhio** lō'kyō

9

217

face	**la faccia** lä fä'tshä	
finger	**il dito,** *pl:* **le dita** ēl dē'tō, *pl:* le dē'tä	
foot	**il piede** ēl pye'de	
forehead	**la fronte** lä frōn'te	
gall bladder	**la bile** lä bē'le	
genitals	**gli organi genitali** lyē ōr'gänē jenētä'lē	
gland	**la ghiandola** lä gyän'dōlä	
hand	**la mano** lä mä'nō	
head	**la testa** lä te'stä	
heart	**il cuore** ēl kōō·ō're	
hip	**l'anca** län'kä	
intestine	**l'intestino** lēntestē'nō	
joint	**l'articolazione** *f* lärtēkōlätsyō'ne	
kidney	**il rene** ēl re'ne	
knee	**il ginocchio** ēl jēnō'kyō	
–cap	**la rotula** lä rō'tōōlä	
leg	**la gamba** lä gäm'bä	
lung	**il polmone** ēl pōlmō'ne	
mouth	**la bocca** lä bō'kä	
muscle	**il muscolo** ēl mōō'skōlō	
neck *(in general)*	**il collo** ēl kō'lō	
neck *(nape)*	**la nuca** lä nōō'kä	
nerve	**il nervo** ēl ner'vō	
nose	**il naso** ēl nä'sō	
pelvis	**il bacino** ēl bätshē'nō	
penis	**il pene** ēl pe'ne	
rib	**la costola** lä kō'stōlä	
–cage	**il torace** ēl tōrä'tshe	
shin	**la tibia** lä tē'byä	

shoulder	**la spalla** lä spä′lä
– blade	**la scapola** lä skä′pōlä
sinus	**il seno frontale** ēl se′nō frōntä′le
skin	**la pelle** lä pe′le
spine	**la spina dorsale** lä spē′nä dōrsä′le
stomach	**lo stomaco** lō stō′mäkō
tendon	**il tendine** ēl ten′dēne
thigh	**la coscia** lä kō′shä
throat	**la gola** lä gō′lä
thyroid (gland)	**la tiroide** lä tēroē′de
toe	**il dito del piede** ēl dē′tō del pye′de
tongue	**la lingua** lä lēn′gōō·ä
tonsils	**le tonsille** le tōnsē′le
tooth	**il dente** ēl den′te
vagina	**la vagina** lä väje′nä
vein	**la vena** lä ve′nä
vertebra	**la vertebra** lä ver′tebrä

Diseases, Doctor, Hospital

9

abscess	**l'ascesso** läshe′sō
Aids	**l'Aids** *m* läēds
allergy	**l'allergia** lälerjē′ä
appendicitis	**l'appendicite** *f* läpendētshē′te
asthma	**l'asma** läz′mä
bite	**il morso** ēl mōr′sō
blister	**la vescica** lä veshē′kä
blood	**il sangue** ēl sän′gōō·e
blood poisoning	**la setticemia** lä setētsheme′ä

219

blood pressure	**la pressione (sanguigna)**
	lä presyō′ne (sän·gōō·ē′nyä)
high –	**la pressione alta**
	lä presyō′ne äl′tä
low –	**la pressione bassa** lä presyō′ne bä′sä
blood transfusion	**la trasfusione (del sangue)**
	lä träsfōōzyō′ne (del sän′gōō·e)
blood type	**il gruppo sanguigno**
	ēl grōō′po sän·gōō·ē′nyō
broken	**rotto** rō′tō
bruise	**la contusione** lä kōntōōzyō′ne
burn	**l'ustione** *f* lōōstyō′ne
cardiac arrest	**l'infarto** lēnfär′tō
certificate	**il certificato** ēl tshertēfēkä′tō
chicken pox	**la varicella** lä värētshe′lä
circulation	**i disturbi circolatori**
problems	ē dēstōōr′bē tshērkōlätō′rē
cold	**il raffreddore** ēl räfredō′re
colic	**la colica** lä kō′lēkä
concussion	**la commozione cerebrale**
	lä kōmōtsyō′ne tsherebrä′le
conjunctivitis	**la congiuntivite** lä kōnjōōntēvē′te
cough	**la tosse** lä to′se
cramp	**il crampo** ēl kräm′pō
cystitis	**la cistite** lä tshēstē′te
dermatologist	**il dermatologo** ēl dermätō′lōgō
diabetes	**il diabete** ēl dyäbe′te
diarrhea	**la diarrea** lä dyärē′ä
dislocated	**lussato** lōōsä′tō

dizziness	**le vertigini** le vertē'jēnē	
doctor *(male)*	**il dottore, il medico**	
	ēl dōtō're, ēl me'dēkō	
doctor *(female)*	**la dottoressa** lä dōtōre'sä	
ear infection	**l'otite *f* media** lōtē'te me'dyä	
ear, nose and throat doctor	**l'otorinolaringoiatra**	
	lōtōrēnōlärēn·gōyä'trä	
faint *(feeling)*	**svenuto** zvenōō'tō	
feces	**le feci** le fe'tshē	
fever	**la febbre** lä fe'bre	
flu	**l'influenza** lēnflōō·en'tsä	
food poisoning	**l'intossicazione *f* da alimenti**	
	lēntōsēkätsyō'ne dä älēmen'tē	
fungal infection	**la micosi** lä mēkōsē	
gallstones	**i calcoli biliari** ē käl'kōlē bēlēä'rē	
general practitioner	**il medico generico** ēl me'dēkō jene'rēkō	
German measles	**la rosolia** lä rōzōlē'ä	
gynecologist *(female)*	**la ginecologa** lä jēnekō'lōgä	
gynecologist *(male)*	**il ginecologo** ēl jēnekō'lōgō	
hay fever	**il raffreddore da fieno**	
	ēl räfredō're dä fye'nō	
headache	**il mal di testa** ēl mäl dē te'stä	
heart	**il cuore** ēl kōō'ō'ro	
– attack	**l'attacco cardiaco** lätä'kō kärdē'akō	
– burn	**i bruciori di stomaco**	
	ē brōōtshō're dē stō'mäkō	

– defect	**il difetto cardiaco** ēl dēfe'tō kärdē'äkō
hemorrhage	**l'emorragia** le mōräje'ä
hernia	**l'ernia inguinale** ler'në-ä ēngōō-ënä'le
herpes	**l'herpes** *m* ler'pes
illness	**la malattia** lä mälätē'ä
infection	**l'infezione** *f* lēnfetsyō'ne
infectious	**contagioso** kōntäjō'sō
inflammation	**l'infiammazione** *f* lēnfyämätsyō'ne
injury	**la ferita** lä ferē'tä
internist	**l'internista** *m, f* lēnternē'stä
kidney stones	**i calcoli renali** ē käl'kōlē renä'lē
lumbago	**la lombaggine** lä lōmbä'jēne
measles	**il morbillo** ēl mōrbē'lō
migraine	**l'emicrania** lemēkrä'nēä
mumps	**gli orecchioni** *m/pl* lyē ōrekyō'nē
nausea	**la nausea** lä nou'ze-ä
nose bleed	**l'emorragia nasale** lemōräje'ä näsä'le
nurse	**l'infermiera** lēnfermye'rä
to operate	**operare** ōperä're
ophthalmologist	**l'oculista** *m* lōkōōlē'stä
orthopedist	**l'ortopedico** lōrtōpe'dēkō
pain(s)	**i dolori** *m/pl* ē dōlō'rē
pediatrician	**il pediatra** ēl pedyä'trä
pneumonia	**la polmonite** lä pōlmōnē'te
poisoning	**l'avvelenamento** lävelenämen'tō
polio	**la poliomielite** lä pōlēomēelē'te
pregnant	**incinta** ēntshēn'tä
pulled muscle	**lo stiramento** lō stērämen'tō

222

pulled tendon	**lo stiramento (dei tendini)**
	lō stērämen'tō (de'ē ten'dēnē)
pus	**il pus** ēl pōōs
rash	**l'esantema** *m* lēsänte'mä
respiratory	**le difficoltà respiratorie**
problems	le dēfēkōltä' respērätōr'ye
rheumatism	**i reumatismi** *m/pl* ē rc·ōōmätēz'mē
scarlet fever	**la scarlattina** lä skärläte'nä
sciatica	**la sciatica** lä shä'tēkä
seasickness	**il mal di mare** ēl mäl dē mä're
the shivers	**i brividi (di febbre)** ē brē'vēdē (dē fe'bre)
shock	**lo shock** lō shōk
sinus infection	**la sinusite** lä sēnōōze'te
sore throat	**il mal di gola** ēl mäl dē gō'lä
sprained	**slogato** zlōgä'tō
sting	**la puntura** lä pōōntōō'rä
stomachache	**il mal di stomaco** ēl mäl dē stō'mäkō
stomach ulcer	**l'ulcera gastrica** lōōl'tsherä gä'strekä
stroke	**il colpo apoplettico** ēl kōl'pō äpōple'tēkō
sunstroke	**l'insolazione** *f* lēnsōlätsyō'ne
sunburn	**la scottatura (da sole)**
	lä skōtätōō'rä (dä sō'le)
sweating	**la forte traspirazione**
	lä fōr'te träspērätsyō'ne
swelling	**il gonfiore** ēl gōnfyō're
tetanus	**il tetano** ēl te'tänō
tonsillitis	**la tonsillite** lä tōnsēlē'te
torn ligament	**lo strappo ai legamenti**
	lō strä'pō ī legämen'tē

ulcer	**l'ulcera** lōōl'tsherä
urine sample	**l'analisi _f_ delle urine**
	länä'lēsē de'le ōōrē'ne
urologist	**l'urologo** lōōrō'lōgō
vaccination	**la vaccinazione** lä vätshēnätsyō'ne
– record	**il libretto delle vaccinazioni**
	ēl lēbre'tō de'le vätshēnätsyō'nē
venereal disease	**la malattia venerea** lä mälätē'ä vene're-ä
veterinarian	**il veterinario** ēl veterēnär'yō
vomiting	**il vomito** ēl vō'mētō
ward	**il reparto** ēl repär'tō
whooping cough	**la pertosse** lä pertō'se
wound	**la ferita** lä ferē'tä
to X-ray	**fare una radiografia**
	fä're ōō'nä rädyōgräfe'ä

At the Dentist's

… hurts.	**Mi fa male …** mē fä mä'le …
This tooth here	**questo dente.** kōō-e'stō den'te.
This tooth at the top	**il dente qui sopra.** ēl den'te kōō-ē' sō'prä.
This tooth at the bottom	**il dente qui sotto.** ēl den'te kōō-ē' sō'tō.
This tooth on the right	**il dente qui a destra.** ēl den'te kōō-ē' ä des'trä.
This tooth on the left	**il dente qui a sinistra.** ēl den'te kōō-ē' ä sēnēs'trä.

This tooth is broken.	**Mi si è rotto questo dente.** mē sē e rō'tō kōō·e'stō den'te.
I've lost a filling.	**È andata via l'otturazione.** e ändä'tä vē'ä lōtōōrätsyō'ne.
Can you do a temporary job on the tooth?	**Può fare soltanto un trattamento provvisorio?** pōō·ō' fä're sōltän'tō ōōn trätämen'tō prōvēzōr'yō?
Please don't pull the tooth.	**Non mi tolga il dente, per favore.** nōn mē tōl'gä ēl den'te, per fävō're.
Would you give me/I'd rather not have an injection, please.	***Mi faccia/Non mi faccia*** la puntura. mē fä'tshä/nōn mē fä'tshä lä pōōntōō'rä.

What the dentist says

Occorre ... ōkō're ...

un ponte. ōōn pōn'te.	You need a ...
un'otturazione. ōōnōtōōrätsyō'ne.	bridge.
una corona. ōō'nä kōrō'nä.	filling. crown.

Devo estrarre il dente.
de'vō esträ're ēl den'te.

I'll have to pull the tooth.

Si sciacqui bene la bocca.
sē shä'kōō·ē be'ne lä bō'kä.

Rinse out your mouth, please.

Non mangi niente per due ore.
nōn män'jē nēen'te per dōō'e ō're.

Don't eat anything for two hours.

9

(local) anesthetic	**l'anestesia (locale)** länesteze̅'ä (lōkä'le)
braces	**l'apparecchio per i denti** läpäre'kyō per ē den'tē
bridge	**il ponte** ēl pōn'te
cavity	**la carie** lä kär'ye̅
collar of the tooth	**il collo del dente** ēl kō'lō del den'te
crown	**la corona** lä kōrō'nä
gold –	**la corona d'oro** lä kōrō'nä dō'rō
porcelain –	**la corona di porcellana** lä kōrō'nä dē pōrtshelä'nä
dentist	**il dentista** ēl dentē'stä
dentures	**la dentiera, la protesi** lä dentye'rä, lä prōte'zē
eye tooth	**il (dente) canino** ēl (den'te) känē'nō
filling	**l'otturazione** *f* lōtōōrätsyō'ne
amalgam –	**l'otturazione** *f* **di amalgama** lōtōōrätsyō'ne dē ämäl'gämä
synthetic –	**l'otturazione di materiale sintetico** lōtōōrätsyō'ne dē mäteryä'le sēnte'tēkō
gums	**la gengiva** lä jenjē'vä
gum disease	**la paradentosi** lä pärädentō'zē
imprint	**il calco** ēl käl'kō
incisor	**il dente incisivo** ēl den'te ēntshēzē'vō
inflammation	**l'infiammazione** *f* lēnfyämätsyō'ne
injection	**la puntura** lä pōōntōō'rä
inlay	**l'otturazione d'oro** lōtōōrätsyō'ne dō'rō
jaw	**la mascella** lä mäshe'lä

molar	**il (dente) molare** ēl (den'te) mōlä're
nerve	**il nervo** ēl ner'vō
office hours	**l'orario delle visite** lōrär'yō de'le vē'zēte
orthodontal clinic	**la clinica odontoiatrica** lä klē'nēkä ōdōntōyä'trēkä
pivot tooth	**il dente a perno** ēl den'te ä per'nō
to pull	**estrarre** esträ're
root	**la radice** lä rädē'tshe
– canal work	**il trattamento della radice** ēl trätämen'tō de'lä rädē'tshe
tooth	**il dente** ēl den'te
– decay	**la carie** lä kär'ye
wisdom tooth	**il dente del giudizio** ēl den'te del jōōdē'tsyō

POLICE; LOST AND FOUND

Where is the nearest police station?	**Dov'è il posto di polizia più vicino?** dōve' ēl pō'stō dē pōlētsē'ä pyōō vētshē'nō?

INFO The police in Italy are divided into three forces: the **carabinieri** käräbēnye'rē, the **polizia** pōlētsē'ä, and the **vigili urbani** vē'jēlē ōōrbä'nē. The **vigili urbani** are responsible for traffic and the stores in the towns. The **polizia** and the **carabinieri** have almost identical duties, but the **carabinieri** work under the auspices of the military, and the **polizia** answer to the civil authorities.

Does anyone here speak English?	**C'è qualcuno che parla inglese?** tshe kōō·älkōō'nō ke pär'lä ēn·gle'se?
I'd like to report ...	**Vorrei denunciare ...** vōre'ē denōōntshä're ...
a theft.	**un furto.** ōōn fōōr'tō.
an accident.	**un incidente.** ōōn ēntshēden'te.
a rape.	**uno stupro.** ōō'nō stōō'prō.
My *daughter/son* has disappeared.	*Mia figlia/Mio figlio* è ♀ **scomparsa/** ♂ **scomparso.** mē'ä fē'lyä/mē'ō fē'lyō e ♀ skōmpär'sä/♂ skōmpär'sō.
My ... has been stolen.	**Mi hanno rubato ...** mē ä'nō rōōbä'tō ...
I've lost ...	**Ho perso ...** ō per'sō ...
My car has been broken into.	**Hanno forzato la mia macchina.** ä'nō fōrtsä'tō lä mē'ä mä'kēnä.
My *room/house* has been broken into.	**Qualcuno è etrato nella mia *casa/ camera.*** kōō·älkōō'nō e eträ'tō ne'lä mē'ä kä'sä/kä'merä.
I need a copy of the official report for insurance purposes.	**Mi occorre una copia della denuncia per la mia assicurazione.** mē ōkō're ōō'nä kō'pyä de'lä denōōn'tshä per lä mē'ä äsēkōōrätsyō'ne.
I'd like to speak to *my lawyer/the consulate.*	**Vorrei parlare con il mio *avvocato/ consolato.*** vōre'ē pärlä're kōn ēl mē'ō ävōkä'tō/kōnsōlä'tō.

228

What the police say

Compili questo modulo, per favore. kömpē'lē kōō·e'stō mō'dōōlō, per fävö're.	Please fill out this form.
I Suoi documenti, per favore. ē sōō·oi' dōkōōmen'tē, per fävö're.	Your passport, please.
Dove abita *in America/qui***?** dō've ä'bētä ēn äme'rēkä/kōō·ē'?	What is your address *in the United States/ here*?
Quando/Dove **è successo?** kōō·än'dō/dō've e sōōtshe'sō?	*When/Where* did this happen?
Si rivolga al Suo consolato, per favore. sē rēvōl'gä äl sōō'ō kōnsōlä'tō, per fävö're.	Please get in touch with your consulate.

Police; Lost and Found

accident	**l'incidente** *m* lēntshēden'te
to arrest	**arrestare** ärestä're
to assault	**picchiare** pēkyä're
broken into	**forzato** förtsä'tō
car	**la macchina** lä mä'kēnä
– key	**le chiavi della macchina** le kyä'vē de'lä mä'kēnä
– radio	**l'autoradio** *f* loutörä'dyō
– registration	**i documenti della macchina** ē dōkōōmen'tē de'lä mä'kēnä
consulate	**il consolato** ēl kōnsōlä'tō

9

229

court (of law)	**il tribunale** ēl trēbōōnä'le
handbag	**la borsa** lä bōr'sä
lawyer *(female)*	**l'avvocatessa** lävōkäte'sä
lawyer *(male)*	**l'avvocato** lävōkä'to
lost	**perso** per'sō
– and found	**l'ufficio oggetti smarriti** lōōfē'tshō ōje'tē zmärē'tē
mugging	**l'aggressione** *f* lägresyō'ne
passport	**il passaporto** ēl päsäpōr'tō
pickpocket	**lo scippatore** lō shēpätō're
police	**la polizia** lä pōlētsē'ä
–man	**il poliziotto** ēl pōlētsyō'tō
– station	**il posto di polizia** ēl pō'stō dē pōlētsē'ä
–woman	**la poliziotta** lä pōlētsyō'tä
prison	**la prigione** lä prējō'ne
purse	**il portamonete** ēl pōrtämōne'te
rape	**lo stupro** lō stōō'prō
to report *(someone/ something)* to the police	**denunciare** denōōntshä're
stolen	**rubato** rōōbä'tō
theft	**il furto** ēl fōōr'tō
thief	**il ladro** ēl lä'drō
witness	**il testimone** ēl testēmō'ne

Time and Weather

Time of Day

What time is it?	**Che ore sono?** ke ō're sō'nō?
It's one o'clock.	**È l'una.** e lōō'nä.
It's two o'clock.	**Sono le due.** sō'nō le dōō·e.
It's twelve *noon/ midnight*.	**È mezzogiorno/mezzanotte.** e *metsōjōr'nō/metsänō'te.*
It's twenty-five minutes to four.	**Sono le tre e trentacinque.** sō'nō le tre e trentätshēn'kōō·e.
It's a quarter past five.	**Sono le cinque e un quarto.** sō'nō le tshēn'kōō·e e ōōn kōō·är'tō.
It's six-thirty.	**Sono le sei e mezza.** sō'nō le se'ē e me'tsä.
It's a quarter to nine.	**Sono le nove meno un quarto.** sō'nō le nō've me'nō ōōn kōō·är'tō.
It's five after four.	**Sono le quattro e cinque.** sō'nō le kōō·ä'trō e tshēn'kōō·e.
It's ten to eight.	**Sono le otto meno dieci.** sō'nō le ō'tō me'nō dye'tshē.
(At) What time?	**A che ora?** ä ke ō'rä?
At (about) eleven.	**Alle undici (circa).** ä'le ōōn'dētshē (tshēr'kä).

From eight to nine (o'clock).	**Dalle otto alle nove.** dä'le ō'tō ä'le nō've.
Until 11 o'clock.	**Fino alle undici.** fē'nō ä'le ōōn'dētshē.
Between ten and twelve.	**Tra le dieci e mezzogiorno.** trä le dye'tshē e metsōjōr'nō.
Not before seven p.m.	**Non prima delle sette (di sera).** nōn prē'mä de'le se'te (dē se'rä).
Shortly after nine.	**Poco dopo le nove.** pō'kō dō'pō le nō've.
Around seven.	**Verso le sette.** ver'sō le se'te.
In half an hour.	**Fra mezz'ora.** frä metsō'rä.
It's (too) late.	**È (troppo) tardi.** e (trō'pō) tär'dē.

Basic Vocabulary

afternoon	**il pomeriggio** ēl pōmerē'jo
in the –	**di pomeriggio** dē pōmerē'jo
ago	**fa** fä
at	**a**, *pl:* **alle** ä, *pl:* ä'le
– three o'clock	**alle tre** ä'le tre
before	**prima** prē'mä
day	**il giorno** ēl jōr'nō
during the –	**di giorno** dē jōr'nō
earlier	**prima** prē'mä
early	**presto** pre'stō
evening	**la sera** lä se'rä

10

233

in the –	**di sera**	dē se'rä
this –	**stasera**	stäse'rä
every half hour	**ogni mezz'ora**	ō'nyē metsō'rä
for	**da**	dä
hour	**l'ora**	lō'rä
half an –	**mezz'ora**	metsō'rä
quarter of an –	**il quarto d'ora**	ēl kōō·är'tō dō'rä
in/on time	**in tempo**	ēn tem'pō
late	**tardi**	tär'dē
later	**più tardi**	pyōō tär'dē
minute	**il minuto**	ēl mēnōō'tō
month	**il mese**	ēl me'se
a – ago	**un mese fa**	ōōn me'se fä
morning	**la mattina**	lä mätē'nä
in the –	**di mattina**	dē mätē'nä
this –	**stamattina**	stämätē'nä
night	**la notte**	lä nō'te
at –	**di notte**	dē nō'te
noon	**il mezzogiorno**	ēl metsōjōr'nō
at –	**a mezzogiorno**	ä metsōjōr'nō
now	**adesso**	äde'sō
season	**la stagione**	lä stäjō'ne
second	**il secondo**	ēl sekōn'dō
since	**da**	dä
sometimes	**qualche volta**	kōō·ä'lke vōl'tä
soon	**presto**	pre'stō
today	**oggi**	ō'jē
tomorrow	**domani**	dōmä'nē
the day after –	**dopodomani**	dōpōdōmä'nē

234

tonight	**stanotte** stäno'te
until	**fino** fē'nō
week	**la settimana** lä setēmä'nä
every –	**ogni settimana** ō'nyē setēmä'nä
weekly	**settimanale** setēmänä'le
year	**l'anno** lä'nō
last –	**l'anno scorso** lä'nō skôr'sō
next –	**l'anno prossImo** lä'nō prō'sēmō
yesterday	**ieri** ē·e'rē

Seasons

spring	**la primavera** lä prēmäve'rä
summer	**l'estate** *f* lestä'te
fall	**l'autunno** lautōō'nō
winter	**l'inverno** lēnver'nō

Legal Holidays

Mardi gras	**il carnevale** ēl kärnevä'le
Good Friday	**il Venerdì Santo** ēl venerdē sän'tō
Easter	**la Pasqua** lä päs'kōō·ä
Pentecost	**la Pentecoste** lä pentekō'ste
Assumption of Mary	**l'Assunzione, il Ferragosto** läsōōntsyō'ne, ēl ferägō'sto
Christmas Eve	**la vigilia di Natale** lä vēje'lēä dē nätä'le
Christmas	**il Natale** ēl nätä'le
New Year	**il Capodanno** ēl käpōdä'nō
New Year's Eve	**San Silvestro** sän sēlves'trō

10

235

The feast day of each town's or city's patron saint is a holiday there; for example, June 24 is a holiday in Florence, June 29, in Rome, etc. **La Liberazione** (Italian Independence Day) is observed on April 25, but there are usually no special celebrations on that day.

THE DATE

What's today's date?	**Quanti ne abbiamo oggi?** kōō·än'tē ne äbyä'mō ō'jē?
Today is July 2nd.	**Oggi è il due luglio.** ō'jē e ēl dōō'e lōō'lyō.
We're leaving on August 20th.	**Partiamo il venti agosto.** pärtyä'mō ēl ven'tē ägō'stō.

Days of the Week

Monday	**lunedì** lōōnedē'
Tuesday	**martedì** märtedē'
Wednesday	**mercoledì** merkōledē'
Thursday	**giovedì** jovedē'
Friday	**venerdì** venerdē'
Saturday	**sabato** sä'bätō
Sunday	**domenica** dōme'nēkä

INFO The first day of the month is designated by an ordinal number; for example **primo luglio** prē'mō lōō'lyō (the first of June).

Months

January	**gennaio** jenä'yō
February	**febbraio** febrä'yō
March	**marzo** mär'tso
April	**aprile** äprē'le
May	**maggio** mä'jō
June	**giugno** jōō'nyō
July	**luglio** lōō'lyō
August	**agosto** ägō'stō
September	**settembre** setem'bre
October	**ottobre** ōtō'bre
November	**novembre** nōvem'bre
December	**dicembre** dētshem'bre

THE WEATHER

What's the weather going to be like today?	**Che tempo farà oggi?** ke tem'pō färä' ō'jē?
Have you heard the weather forecast yet?	**Ha già sentito le previsioni del tempo?** ä jä sentē'tō le prevēsyō'nē del tem'pō?
It's/It's going to be …	**Fa/Farà …** fä/färä' …
warm.	**caldo.** käl'dō.
hot.	**molto caldo.** mōl'tō käl'dō.
cold.	**freddo.** fre'dō.
cool.	**fresco.** fre'skō
It's humid.	**C'è afa.** tshe ä'fä.

10

237

It's rather windy.	**Tira parecchio vento.**	
	të′rä päre′kyō ven′tō.	
It's very windy.	**C'è molto vento.** tshe mōl′tō ven′tō.	
The sky is *clear/ cloudy*.	**Il cielo è *sereno/nuvoloso*.**	
	ēl tshe′lō e *sere′nō/nōōvōlō′zō*.	
What's the temperature?	**Quanti gradi ci sono?**	
	kōō·än′tē grä′dē tshe sō′nō?	
It's … degrees (below zero).	**Ci sono … gradi (sotto zero).**	
	tshē sō′nō … grä′dē (sō′tō dze′rō).	
It looks like *rain/ a storm*.	**Pare che voglia *piovere/fare un temporale*.** pä′re ke vō′lyä *pyō′vere/fä′re ōōn tempōrä′le*.	
It's foggy.	**C'è nebbia.** tshe ne′byä.	
The streets are icy.	**Le strade sono ghiacciate.**	
	le strä′de sō′nō gyätshä′te.	

The Weather

air	**l'aria** lär′yä	
clear	**sereno, limpido** sere′nō, lēm′pēdō	
climate	**il clima** ēl klē′mä	
cloud	**la nuvola** lä nōō′vōlä	
–burst	**il nubifragio** ēl nōōbēfrä′jō	
cloudy	**nuvoloso** nōōvōlō′zō	
cold	**freddo** fre′dō	
I'm –	**sento freddo** sen′tō fre′dō	

238

cool	**fresco** fre'skō	
damp	**umido** ōō'mēdō	
dawn	**l'alba** läl'bä	
degree	**il grado** ēl grä'dō	
drizzle	**la pioviggine** lä pyōvējē'ne	
dry	**secco** se'kō	
dusk	**il crepuscolo** ēl krepōōs'kōlō	
fair	**sereno** sere'nō	
fog	**la nebbia** lä ne'byä	
frost	**il gelo** ēl je'lō	
heat	**il caldo** ēl käl'dō	
– wave	**l'ondata di caldo** lōndä'tä dē käl'dō	
high-pressure area	**l'alta pressione** läl'tä presyō'ne	
hot	**(molto) caldo** (mōl'tō) käl'dō	
I'm –	**sento caldo** sen'tō käl'dō	
humid	**afoso** äfō'sō	
ice *(in general)*	**il ghiaccio** ēl gyä'tshō	
ice *(on the road)*	**il gelo** ēl je'lō	
it's freezing	**gela** je'lä	
it's raining	**piove** pyō've	
it's snowing	**nevica** ne'vēkä	
it's thawing	**sgela** sje'lä	
lightning	**i lampi** ē läm'pē	
low-pressure area	**la bassa pressione** lä bä'sä presyō'ne	
moon	**la luna** lä lōō·nä	
overcast	**coperto** kōper'tō	
rain	**la pioggia** lä pyō'jä	
rainy	**piovoso** pyōvō'zō	

10

239

shower	**il rovescio di pioggia**
	ēl rōveˈshō dē pyōˈjä
snow	**la neve** lä neˈve
star	**la stella** lä steˈlä
storm	**la tempesta** lä tempeˈstä
stormy	**tempestoso** tempestōˈsō
sun	**il sole** ēl sōˈle
–rise	**il sorgere del sole** ēl sōrˈjere del sōˈle
–set	**il tramonto** ēl trämōnˈtō
sunny	**soleggiato** sōlejäˈtō
temperature	**la temperatura** lä temperätōōˈrä
thaw	**il disgelo** ēl dēsjeˈlō
thunder	**il tuono** ēl tōō-ōˈnō
–storm	**il temporale** ēl tempōräˈle
variable	**variabile** väryäˈbēle
warm	**caldo** kälˈdō
weather	**il tempo** ēl temˈpō
–forecast	**il bollettino meteorologico**
	ēl bōleēˈnō mete-ōrōlōˈjēkō
wet	**bagnato** bänyäˈtō
wind	**il vento** ēl venˈtō
east –	**il vento di levante**
	ēl venˈtō dē levänˈte
north –	**la tramontana** lä trämōntäˈnä
south –	**il vento australe** ēl venˈtō ousträˈle
west –	**il vento di ponente**
	ēl venˈtō dē pōnenˈte
–force	**la forza del vento** lä fōrˈtsä del venˈtō
windy	**ventoso** ventōˈsō

Grammar

ARTICLES

Definite Articles

As with most other foreign languages, Italian divides nouns into genders: nouns, their preceeding articles and accompanying adjectives are either *masculine* or *feminine*.

	Singular	Plural
♂	il	i
♂ in front of **s + consonant, z, gn** e. g. **lo studente** the student	lo	gli
♀	la	le

When the articles **il** and **la** are coupled with a noun beginning with a vowel, they are abbreviated to **l'**: for example **l'amica** – the (female) friend, **l'amico** – the (male) friend.

When referring to someone in the third person by their last name, the definite article must precede **signor(e)** or **signora**: **la signora Rossi** – Mrs. Rossi. If, however, you are addressing someone, **signor** and **signora** are used without an article: **Come sta, signor Ferrari?** – How are you, Mr. Ferrari?

The prepositions **a**, **da**, **di**, **in** and **su**, when used together with the articles, are contracted into the following forms:

	il	**lo**	**la**	**l'**
di from, of	**del**	**dello**	**della**	**dell'**
a at, on	**al**	**allo**	**alla**	**all'**
da at, from	**dal**	**dallo**	**dalla**	**dall'**
in in, to	**nel**	**nello**	**nella**	**nell'**
su on	**sul**	**sullo**	**sulla**	**sull'**

	i	**gli**	**le**
di from, of	**dei**	**degli**	**delle**
a at, on	**ai**	**agli**	**alle**
da at, from	**dai**	**dagli**	**dalle**
in in, to	**nei**	**negli**	**nelle**
su on	**sui**	**sugli**	**sulle**

The Indefinite Article

♂	**un**
♂ in front of **s + consonant**, **z**, **gn** e. g. **uno studente** a student	**uno**
♀	**una**

Partitive Articles and Amounts

If you wish to describe an indefinite amount or number, you must use the "partitive article". It is formed by putting the preposition **di** together with the respective definite article: **Ho comprato delle arance.** – I have bought (some) oranges.

On the other hand, if you wish to denote a definite amount, you must couple the noun itself with **di**: **un piatto di spaghetti** – a plate of spaghetti, **un litro di latte** – a liter of milk. The expression **un po'** (a bit of) also counts as a definite amount: **un po' di formaggio** – a bit of cheese.

NOUNS

Nouns ending in **-o** are almost always masculine; nouns ending in **-a** are almost always feminine. Nouns ending in **-e** can be either masculine or feminine.

Plurals in Italian are formed in different ways and depend upon the gender and ending of the noun. The following table shows how to put singular nouns into the plural:

	Singular	Plural
♂ (-o)	**il ragazzo** the boy	**i ragazzi** the boys
♀ (-a)	**la ragazza** the girl	**le ragazze** the girls
♂ oder ♀	**il padre** the father	**i padri** the fathers
(-e)	**la madre** the mother	**le madri** the mothers

The few masculine nouns that end in **-a** use the **-i** ending when in the plural: **il problema** – the problem → **i problemi**.

Special cases:

1. In order to retain the same pronunciation of the letters **c** and **g**, words that end in **-co** or **-ca** and **-go** or **-ga** take on an **h** be-

fore the **-i** or **-e** ending: **bianco** – white → **bianchi**, **amica** – (female) friend → **amiche**. There are exceptions to this rule: **amico** – (male) friend → **amici**; and words ending in **-co** and **-go** whose emphasis falls on the third-to-last syllable: **medico** – doctor → **medici**.

2. Most nouns ending in **-cia** and **-gia** lose the **-i-** when in the plural: **spiaggia** - beach → **spiagge**.

3. Most nouns ending in **-io** form the plural only with *one* **-i**: **viaggio** – journey, trip → **viaggi**.

ADJECTIVES AND ADVERBS

Adjectives

Adjectives conform in gender and number to the nouns they are modifying.

If the masculine adjective form ends in an **-o**, then the feminine form of that adjective will substitute an **-a** for the **-o**: **piccolo** – small → **piccola**. Adjectives ending in **-e** have the same endings for both genders. To make the plural, the same rules as for nouns apply.

Adjectives usually come after the noun in Italian: **la macchina rossa** – the red car. Some adjectives may, however, come before the noun.

If an adjective describes a place of origin, it will be written in lower case: **la cucina italiana** – Italian cuisine.

Special cases:

1. When used before masculine singular nouns that do not begin with a z, gn or an s + consonant, the word **"buono"** (good) will be shortened into **buon: un buon ristorante** – a good restaurant.

2. When used before singular nouns that do not begin with a z, **gn**, vowel or s + consonant, the word **"grande"** (large) will be shortened into **gran: una gran festa** – a large festival.

Comparatives

Adjectives are intensified for the comparative by putting **più** in front of them. To form the superlative, **più** is used with the definite article: **bello** – beautiful → **più bello** – more beautiful → **il più bello** – most beautiful.

È più bello sciare che nuotare. Skiing is nicer than swimming.
È più giovane di me. He/She is younger than I.

To express "very" + adjective, the suffix **-issimo** or **-issima** is used: **Roma è bellissima.** Rome is very beautiful.

Adverbs

Adverbs are made by adding the suffix **"-mente"** to the feminine form of the adjective, for example:
tranquillo quiet → **tranquilla** → **tranquillamente** quietly
felice happy → **felicemente** happily.

If the adjective ends in **-le** or **-re**, it loses the **-e** before adding **-mente**: **piacevole** pleasant → **piacevolmente** pleasantly.

Comparatives

Adverbs form the comparative like the adjectives: **presto** early → **più presto** earlier → **al più presto** at the earliest → **prestissimo** very early.

PRONOUNS

Personal Pronouns

	Nominative		Dative		Accusative	
Singular	**io**	I	**mi**	(to) me	**mi**	me
	tu	you	**ti**	(to) you	**ti**	you
	lui	he	**gli**	(to) him	**lo**	him
	lei	she	**le**	(to) her	**la**	her
	Lei	you	**Le**	(to) you	**La**	you
		(polite)		*(polite)*		*(polite)*
Plural	**noi**	we	**ci**	(to) us	**ci**	us
	voi	you	**vi**	(to) you	**vi**	you
	Voi	you	**Vi**	(to) you	**Vi**	you
		(polite)		*(polite)*		*(polite)*
	loro	they	**gli/loro**	(to) them	**li/le**	them
	Loro	you	**Loro**	(to) you	**Loro**	you
		(polite)		*(polite)*		*(polite)*

The pronouns **la** and **lo** turn into **l'** when preceding a vowel or an **h**: **l'abbiamo visto** – we have seen him; **l'abbiamo vista** – we have seen her.

247

Note: If you are using the polite form in speaking to someone, then use **Lei** as shown with the third person singular. If you are speaking to more than one person with whom you would use the polite form, then you may use either **Voi** as shown with the second person plural or **Loro** as shown with the third person plural.

You only use the nominative of the personal pronoun if emphasizing a particular person; otherwise the verb ending is sufficient to identify the subject of the action in the sentence: **Sono stanco.** – *I* am tired. **È a casa?** – Is *he/she* at home? (or "Are *you* at home?" in the polite form).

Reflexive Pronouns

The reflexive pronouns are the same in the dative and accusative: **mi**, **ti**, **si**, **ci**, **vi** and **si**.

Ci and Ne

Ci can replace phrases that begin with **a** and **in**: **Sei già stato *a Firenze/in Italia*?** – Have you ever been to Florence/Italy?
Si, ci sono stato. – Yes, I've been there.

Ne can replace phrases that begin with **di** or **da**: **Siete contenti dell'albergo?** – Are you happy with your hotel?
Si, ne siamo contenti. – Yes, we're happy with it.

Pronoun Placement

Pronouns come before a conjugated verb: **Le telefono.** I'll phone you.

Used with the infinitive or imperative verb forms, pronouns are added to the end of the verb to which they apply: **Mi fa piacere rivederLa.** I am happy to see you again.

If more than one pronoun is being used, then the dative pronoun preceeds the accusative. The pronouns **mi, ti, ci, vi** and **si** change correspondingly to **me, te, ce, ve, se: Ve lo do.** – I am giving it to you.

Gli plus **lo, la, le, li** and **ne** are combined as follows: **glielo, gliela, gliele, glieli** and **gliene: Glielo dico.** – I'll say it to him/her.

Possessive Pronouns

possession	Singular		Plural	
possessor	♂	♀	♂	♀
Singular	**il mio**	**la mia**	**i miei**	**le mie**
	il tuo	**la tua**	**i tuoi**	**le tue**
	il suo	**la sua**	**i suoi**	**le sue**
	il Suo	**la Sua**	**i Suoi**	**le Sue**
Plural	**il nostro**	**la nostra**	**i nostri**	**le nostre**
	il vostro	**la vostra**	**i vostri**	**le vostre**
	il loro	**la loro**	**i loro**	**le loro**

You must put the appropriate definite article in front of possessive pronouns: **il mio libro** – my book; **Di chi è questo libro? È (il) mio.** – To whom does this book belong? It belongs to me.

Exception: close relations in the singular: for example **mio fratello** – my brother.

Relative Pronouns

The relative pronoun **che** is used for both genders in nominative and accusative, singular and plural.

With prepositions **cui** is used: **la signora con cui lavoro** – the woman with whom I work.

VERBS

Present Tense

Italian verbs are grouped according to their infinitive endings. They are conjugated more extensively than in English, as you can see from the following table:

	-are lavorare work	-ere prendere take	-ire sentire hear	preferire prefer
(io)	lavor*o*	prend*o*	sent*o*	prefer*isco*
(tu)	lavor*i*	prend*i*	sent*i*	prefer*isci*
(lui)				
(lei)	lavor*a*	prend*e*	sent*e*	prefer*isce*
(Lei)				
(noi)	lavor*iamo*	prend*iamo*	sent*iamo*	prefer*iamo*
(voi)	lavor*ate*	prend*ete*	sent*ite*	prefer*ite*
(loro)	lavor*ano*	prend*ono*	sent*ono*	prefer*iscono*
(Loro)				

Verbs ending in **-care/-gare** insert an **h** before the endings **-i** and **-iamo** in order to maintain the same pronunciation. For example: **cercare** – to look for: **cerco, cerchi, cerca, cerchiamo, cercate, cercano**.

The same rule applies for other verb tenses that use **-e-**, for example the conditional: **cercare → cercherei** – I would look for. Some other verbs conjugated like **preferire** are: **capire** – to understand, **costruire** – to build, **finire** – to finish, **pulire** – to clean, **spedire** – to send, **tossire** – to cough.

avere and *essere*

avere have	**essere** be
ho	**sono**
hai	**sei**
ha	**è**
abbiamo	**siamo**
avete	**siete**
hanno	**sono**

The Perfect Tense

The perfect tense is formed by using the present tense of **avere** or **essere** with a past participle.

The past participle is formed as follows:
1. verbs ending in **-are** use **-ato**: **lavorare → lavorato** – worked
2. verbs ending in **-ere** use **-uto**: **credere** – to believe → **creduto** – believed
3. verbs ending in **-ire** use **-ito**: **sentire → sentito** – heard.

The perfect tense of most verbs is formed using **avere**. If you are using a verb of *motion*, however, the perfect tense is formed with **essere**: ho mangiato – I have eaten; sono andato – I have gone. In addition to verbs of motion, reflexive verbs and some impersonal verbs that usually appear in the third person also form the perfect tense with **essere**: mi sono pettinato – I combed my hair; **mi è piaciuto** – I liked it (translated word-for-word: "It was pleasing to me").

When verbs form the perfect tense with **essere**, the past participle conforms to gender and number just like an adjective: **Laura è uscit*a*. –** Laura has gone out. **I bambini sono andat*i* a giocare. –** The children have gone to play.

When used with **avere**, the past participle only changes when used with the preceding accusative pronouns **lo, la, li, le** and **ne**: **Hai vist*o* Carla? Sì, l'ho vist*a*.** – Have you seen Carla? Yes, I have seen her.

The Conditional

You use the conditional to ask a question or say something politely: **Mi saprebbe dire che ore sono?** – Could you tell me what time it is? **Mi accompagnerebbe a casa?** – Would you take me home? **Vorrei un caffè.** – I would like a (cup of) coffee. The conditional can also express a wish or a possibility: **Vivrei volentieri in Italia.** – I would love to live in Italy.

abitare live	leggere read	uscire go out
abiterei	leggerei	uscirei
abiteresti	leggeresti	usciresti
abiterebbe	leggerebbe	uscirebbe
abiteremmo	leggeremmo	usciremmo
abitereste	leggereste	uscireste
abiterebbero	leggerebbero	uscirebbero

Important irregular verbs

andare go – past participle: **andato**
present tense: **vado, vai, va, andiamo, andate, vanno**
conditional: **andrei** etc.

avere have – past participle: **avuto**
present tense: **ho, hai, ha, abbiamo, avete, hanno**
conditional: **avrei** etc.

bere drink – past participle: **bevuto**
present tense: **bevo, bevi, beve, beviamo, bevete, bevono**
conditional: **berrei** etc.

dare give – past participle: **dato**
present tense: **do, dai, dà, diamo, date, danno**
conditional: **darei** etc.

dire say – past participle: **detto**
present tense: **dico, dici, dice, diciamo, dite, dicono**
conditional: **direi** etc.

dovere have to – past participle: **dovuto**
present tense: **devo, devi, deve, dobbiamo, dovete, devono**
conditional: **dovrei** etc.

essere be – past participle: **stato**
present tense: **sono, sei, è, siamo, siete, sono**
conditional: **sarei** etc.

fare do, make – past participle: **fatto**
present tense: **faccio, fai, fa, facciamo, fate, fanno**
conditional: **farei** etc.

potere can, be able, may – past participle: **potuto**
present tense: **posso, puoi, può, possiamo, potete, possono**
conditional: **potrei** etc.

salire get in – past participle: **salito**
present tense: **salgo, sali, sale, saliamo, salite, salgono**
conditional: **salirei** etc.

sapere know – past participle: **saputo**
present tense: **so, sai, sa, sappiamo, sapete, sanno**
conditional: **saprei** etc.

stare stay – past participle: **stato**
present tense: **sto, stai, sta, stiamo, state, stanno**
conditional: **starei** etc.

tenere hold – past participle: **tenuto**
present tense: **tengo, tieni, tiene, teniamo, tenete, tengono**
conditional: **terrei** etc.

uscire go out – past participle: **uscito**
present tense: **esco, esci, esce, usciamo, uscite, escono**
conditional: **uscirei** etc.

venire come – past participle: **venuto**
present tense: **vengo, vieni, viene, veniamo, venite, vengono**
past tense: venivo etc.

volere want – past participle: **voluto**
present tense: **voglio, vuoi, vuole, vogliamo, volete, vogliono**
conditional: **vorrei** etc.

NEGATIVE SENTENCES

1. no **no**
   Vieni con noi? No, ho da fare. Are you coming will us? No, I'm busy.

2. not **non**
   Non ho mangiato. I haven't eaten.
   Non la compro. I won't buy it.

3. nobody **non … nessuno**
   Non viene nessuno. Nobody comes.

4. nothing **non … niente**
   Non sento niente/nulla. I don't hear anything.

5. never **non … mai**
   Non esco mai. I never go out.

6. not any more **non … più**
   Non lavoro più. I don't work any more.

7. neither … nor **né … né**
   Non mangia né carne né pesce. He eats neither meat nor fish.

255

INTERROGATIVE SENTENCES

When asking questions, place the subject after the verb: **È partito Giovanni?** – Has Giovanni gone? Questions without an interrogative pronoun often retain the same word order as a statement in the indicative; one recognizes the statement as a question by the rising inflection toward the end of the sentence: **Giovanni è partito?** – Has Giovanni gone?

The most important interrogative pronouns

when?	**quando?**	**Quando parte?** When are they leaving?
why?	**perché?**	**Perché non viene?** Why doesn't he come?
what?	**che cosa?**	**Che cosa hai detto?** What did you say?
which?	**quale?**	**Quale vestito ti metti, quello blu?** Which dress are you going to wear, the blue one?
to whom?	**a chi?**	**A chi mandi questo pacco?** To whom are you sending this parcel?
who(m)?	**chi?**	**Chi hai visto?** Whom did you see?
who?	**chi?**	**Chi ti ha scritto?** Who wrote to you?
whose?	**di chi?**	**Di chi è la borsa?** Whose bag is that?
how?	**come?**	**Come si dice?** How do you say that?
how much?	**quanto?**	**Quanto costa?** How much does it cost?
where?	**dove?**	**Dove abita?** Where do you live?
where (from)?	**da dove?**	**Da dove viene?** Where are you from?
where (to)?	**dove?**	**Dove va quest'autobus?** Where does this bus go to?

NUMBERS

Cardinal Numbers

0	**zero**	dze'rō
1	**uno**	ōō'nō
2	**due**	dōō'e
3	**tre**	tre
4	**quattro**	kōō·ä'tro
5	**cinque**	tshēn'kōō·e
6	**sei**	se'ē
7	**sette**	se'te
8	**otto**	ō'tō
9	**nove**	nō've
10	**dieci**	dye'tshē
11	**undici**	ōōn'dētshē
12	**dodici**	dō'dētshē
13	**tredici**	tre'dētshē
14	**quattordici**	kōō ätōr'dētshē
15	**quindici**	kōō·ēn'dētshē
16	**sedici**	se'dētshē
17	**diciasette**	dētshäse'te
18	**diciotto**	dētshō'to
19	**diciannove**	dētshänō've
20	**venti**	ven'tē
21	**ventuno**	ventōō'nō
22	**ventidue**	ventēdōō'e
23	**ventitre**	ventētre'
24	**ventiquattro**	ventēkōō·ä'tro
25	**venticinque**	ventētshēn'kōō·e

26	**ventisei**	ventëse'ē
27	**ventisette**	ventëse'te
28	**ventotto**	ventö'tō
29	**ventinove**	ventēnō've
30	**trenta**	tren'tä
40	**quaranta**	kōō·ärän'tä
50	**cinquanta**	tshēnkōō·än'tä
60	**sessanta**	sesän'tä
70	**settanta**	setän'tä
80	**ottanta**	ōtän'tä
90	**novanta**	nōvän'tä
100	**cento**	tshen'tō
101	**centouno**	tshentō·ōō'nō
200	**duecento**	dōō·etshen'tō
1 000	**mille**	mē'le
2 000	**duemila**	dōō·ēmē'lä
10 000	**diecimila**	dyetshēmē'lä
100 000	**centomila**	tshentomē'lä
1 000 000	**un milione**	ōō mēlyō'ne

Ordinal Numbers

1 st	**primo**	prë'mō
2nd	**secondo**	sekön'dō
3rd	**terzo**	ter'tsō
4th	**quarto**	kōō·är'tō
5th	**quinto**	kōō·ēn'tō
6th	**sesto**	se'stō
7th	**settimo**	se'tēmo
8th	**ottavo**	ōktä'vō